LEROY COLLINS LEON COUNTY PUBLIC LIBRARY
3 1260 01084 1727
W9-BOO-833

Birdie

Confessions of a Baseball Nomad

Birdie Tebbetts with
James Morrison

TRIUMPH
BOOKS
CHICAGO

Copyright © 2002 by James Morrison

No part of this publication may be reproduced, stored in a retrieval system, or transmitted, in any form by any means, electronic, mechanical, photocopying, or otherwise, without the prior written permission of the publisher, Triumph Books, 601 S. LaSalle St., Suite 500, Chicago, IL, 60605.

Library of Congress Cataloging-in-Publication Data

Tebbetts, Birdie, 1912–1999.
Birdie : confessions of a baseball nomad / James Morrison.
p. cm.
ISBN 1-57243-455-4 (hardcover)
1. Tebbetts, Birdie, 1912–1999. 2. Baseball players—United States—Biography. I. Title. II. Morrison, James, 1924– III. Title.

GV865.T33 A3 2002
796.357'092—dc21
[B]

2001055503

This book is available in quantity at special discounts for your group or organization. For further information, contact:
Triumph Books
601 South LaSalle Street
Suite 500
Chicago, Illinois 60605
(312) 939-3330
Fax (312) 663-3557

Printed in the United States of America
ISBN 1-57243-455-4

Interior design by Patricia Frey

B Tebbetts
1084 1727 8/19/02 LCL
Tebbetts, Birdie,
1912-1999.
Birdie : confessions of
a baseball nomad /
KO

LeRoy Collins
Leon County Public Librar
200 W. Park Avenue
Tallahassee, Fl 32301

For Mary

Contents

Foreword

Picture this scene. I had just joined the Yankees. On the first road trip to Los Angeles I came down to the hotel coffee shop for breakfast and there was Birdie Tebbetts, sipping coffee and eating dry toast. Beside him were his two daughters, then in their twenties, who had moved to Los Angeles to seek their fortunes. Birdie winked at me, which I took to be an invitation to join them.

Birdie's job in those days–as master scout for the Yankees–was to travel ahead of the team and work up a scouting report on the opposition. From what I understand he would put it all in writing and hand it over to the manager and then move on to the next city and start all over again.

Now I think it was Thurman Munson who told me to listen when Birdie spoke, because Birdie was one smart old catcher. So while waiting for my ham and eggs and making small talk, I kept wondering how long it would be before we got down to our shared business interest–which was how to hit a slow curve out of the ballpark. Just after the waitress put the plate in front of me and finished pouring more coffee, Birdie asked, "How do you do against Frank Tanana, Reggie?" At that point his daughters rolled their eyes toward the sky and got up and left.

For the next hour I got a firsthand intelligence briefing on how left-hander Tanana was going to pitch to me, and what to expect with men on base, and what to look for with a full count, and on and on he went. I didn't try to remember everything. There was too much. But I helped myself to what I thought I could use and then set out for the ballpark to try to cash it in.

Of course those shrewd insights were not the only reason I felt a special kinship with Birdie. He was also funny. He made you laugh and in those days I needed a laugh and he knew it. He had played, managed, and had been a front office big shot. And now he was a scout. But more than that he was a teacher who respected the ballplayer. He was a fan and I think he had a special place in his heart for great hitters. You have to like a guy who's done it all. And his life story will make you smile.

—Reggie Jackson
January 2002

Acknowledgments

I wish to express my gratitude to a number of persons who have helped me with the preparation of this work.

Appreciation goes first to Ryan Morrison for encouraging me to assemble Birdie's life story.

Thanks to Tom Bast, who suggested a way to approach it.

Needless to say I am grateful to Birdie Tebbetts' four children, George Jr., Betty, Sue, and Pat, for providing the hilarious background on the House of Tebbetts.

Next comes to mind Birdie's sister, Kathryn, a dedicated teacher of America's youth and a lifelong fan of America's pastime. What a nifty combination.

And thanks also to Roland Hemond, who was always available to provide insight into the game, the people who played it, and the deep rumblings in several front offices.

Thanks to Anne Sloan Morrison, who never complained about the clutter and chaos in the writing room.

Finally, my thanks to each of the following, listed in no particular order: Tim McCarver, Bob Howsam, Robert Howsam, Johnny Oates, Paul Hagen, Al Clark, Robert Nassau, Al Rosen, Gene Michaels, Pat Hutchinson, Dave Parker, Ken Carmack, Geoffrey McCullough, Lucy Morrison, Joe Hutchinson, Mark Stangle, Bill James, Roberta Mazur, Joe McDonald, Joe Brown, Bing Devine, Tony Perez, Dave Dombrowskie, Bob Broeg, Al Silverman, Jonathan Diamond, Bill Mitchell, Bob Deluca, Ted

Williams, Hon. Robert Cannon, Nic Antoine, Jax Robertson, John DeLuke, Alex Grammas, Johnny Logan, Gary Hughes, Sam Mele, Ross Legler, Len Sargent, Johnny Pesky, Chuck Hinkel, Rollie Eastwick, Murray Cook, Daniel Boone, Max West, Byron Hollinshead, Rory Johnson, Bob Kaufman, Greg Biagini, Michael Cohen, Peter Fleming, John Daly, John Gallagher, Bob Sann, Mary Frances Sears, Dan Teas, Joe Casey, Josh Hammond, Herman H. Zwinger, Scott Pitoniac, Peter Morrison, Jennifer Unter, Pat Losinski, and the entire staff of the Pikes Peak Library District.

Editorial Note

What you are about to read is the authentic and distinctive voice of George "Birdie" Tebbetts, put down from memory, notes, and recorded conversations that have been edited for clarity, continuity, and context. As editor of this work I take full responsibility for whatever distortions may have arisen due to the editorial process.

My conversations with Birdie took place over the span of the 67 years that I knew him. He died on the 24th of March, 1999. In the two years before that, he and I held lengthy taped discourses about his life and times in baseball. When he was alone he often taped and passed on to me hour-long monologues on aspects of the game. Taken together, that material makes up the body of this work.

During our conversations Birdie would often turn off the recorder and forbid me from taking notes. Birdie was circumspect about what he would say for the record about others, about the baseball establishment, about those whom he obviously disliked.

Birdie is the only known diarist in the history of the major leagues. He kept meticulous and voluminous diaries of almost every working day, going back to his first years with the Detroit organization. The volumes fill an eight-foot shelf. They are largely written in code, which is frequently transparent (for instance, the reference to GS is certainly George Steinbrenner, since Tebbetts was working for him at the time of that writing). These volumes, among several other sources, were indispensable during the writing of this book.

I wish to give special thanks to Birdie's beloved sister, Kathryn Tebbetts, who in his early years looked after Birdie's financial and contractual dealings and whose knowledge of his habits of mind provided a rich source of corroborating detail.

—James Morrison
Colorado Springs, Colorado
February 2002

Introduction

A GAME OF INCHES
Time Magazine, July 8, 1957

Bench-jockeys heckled him from across the diamond and shirtsleeved kibitzers shouted advice from the stands, but the burly, ruddy man alongside the Cincinnati bat rack gave no sign that he heard. The center-field scoreboard reminded him that he was a front-runner in a National League pennant race so close that the loss of a single game might mean the difference between first place and fourth, but beyond pawing abstractedly at his red-sleeved uniform shirt, he appeared unmoved. All week long, alone in the shouting crowd with his furious concentration, the Redlegs manager, George Robert "Birdie" Tebbetts, 44, was busy outguessing the opposition, calling the shots for his own club, and cocking his narrowed, china-blue eyes at the umpires. For a man with so much on his mind, Birdie seemed uncommonly cool and calm.

Birdie Tebbetts may have looked relaxed, but he was simmering inside with the problems, hunches, gambles, and indecision of a competitor who hates to be outguessed, hates even more to lose. He remained squatly in his corner of the bench, not because he was calm but because he was a catcher. As a catcher, he had learned to do his thinking in a crouch. It is a posture that seems to hone the intellect–for catchers, once they have mastered the mask, chest pads, and other "tools of ignorance," seem to make the grade as big-league managers almost as consistently as big-time businessmen make the team on Republican Cabinets. The tradition runs way back to the late Connie Mack and Roger Bresnahan. And from Mr. Mack on through Gabby Street, Mickey Cochrane, and Al Lopez, few major league catchers-turned-manager have matched the swift success of George Robert Tebbetts.

The Redlegs were the sad sacks of the second division when Birdie took them over in 1954; by 1956 they had surprised themselves and come within two games of stealing the pennant. The big difference was Birdie. Sportswriters named him "Manager of the Year," but Cincinnati ball fans amended that, hailing him as "best manager in the majors."

This year the Redlegs are playing like men who really believe they can win–and once more the difference is Birdie. Now, like their manager, the Redlegs are convinced that there is nothing worse in life than losing. So they have bounced back from a staggering last-place start. They have made do without the services of slugger Ted Kluszewski, whose injured back has turned him into a defensive drawback around first base and a spotty performer at the plate. Slowly and steadily they have clawed their way out of recurrent slumps and scrambled back toward the lead, where they are sure they belong.

Without "Big Klu" to flex his muscles and frighten opposing pitchers, every club in the league picked the Redlegs for round-heeled patsies. They had not figured on Birdie Tebbetts. This season's success is not so much a matter of tactics on the field as it is a triumph of Tebbetts' psychology in the clubhouse. Maybe off the diamond the Redlegs will never learn their manager's supreme self-confidence, the positive faith that no man is his superior; maybe some of them sometimes settle for second best–say, in arguments with their wives. But on the ballfield, Birdie has converted them all.

Cincinnati fans knew Birdie as a hustling, 14-year veteran of major league catching. They had heard of him as a scrappy American League catcher (in Detroit, Boston, and Cleveland) who hated to come out second best in anything–a ballgame, an argument with an umpire, a conversation with a friend. They called him "Most Voluble Player in the Majors," but he had had only one short summer of seasoning as a minor-league manager. It was hard to believe that he knew enough tactics to manage a major league club.

Tactics turned out to be the last thing General Manager Gabe Paul was worrying about when he hired Birdie. "You assume that, all the way down to Class D, managers know when to bunt or when to hit-and-run," said Paul. "The important thing is common sense, the ability to handle men." Paul had been thinking of Birdie in terms of those attributes ever since he had read some of Birdie's scouting reports on American Association players. Said Paul, "Anyone who could prepare reports like that had to be a capable and clear-thinking fellow."

Some sample Tebbetts observations:

On a promising pitcher: "Major league stuff and a great arm. Screwy in the head. Eliminate head, and I recommend. Get good surgeon."

On an outfielder: "A low-ball hitter and an off-field hitter. No power; should not be played to pull. He is a good center fielder with a strong arm. A base runner. Every time he bends his left knee toward his right he is stealing."

On a pitcher: "Has major league fastball but is disturbing type on the mound; looks like a mental case."

On another pitcher: "Not recommended on present style. Has major league equipment but is a Thomas Edison [a baseball term for any player who is continually experimenting]."

"Baseball," Birdie told his men, "is exactly what Branch Rickey said it was: 'A race between a man and a ball.' Baseball is a game of inches. A guy catches the ball on the tip of his glove, a batter tops a ball and beats a throw to first. Or a fellow gets up in the ninth and comes through with a liner between third and short–he's a hero. Two inches the other way and he's a bum because he hit into a double play. The only thing you can do is get a little faster man to play each position, keep adding the men who can make the inches work."

Manager-of-the-Year Tebbetts' own popularity impressed him not at all. "If my players like me," he reflects, "it's an accident of personality. I happen to like my players and I treat them like men. I don't know anything about patting one guy on the back and bawling another out. I don't have any doghouses, and I don't deal in personalities. It doesn't make any difference to me if a guy has a good or a bad personality. I play talent. If a guy is not producing and I can't use him, it's not that he's in the doghouse, but that he isn't contributing to the overall picture.

"If a manager doesn't have confidence in his ballplayers, even when they're playing badly, they're not going to have confidence in themselves. And when a ballplayer's confidence is gone, you haven't got a ballplayer–I don't give a damn how great he is. That's why I try never to lose confidence in the best or the least of my players. The rest of it a ballplayer has to do for himself. He takes the bat up to the plate. He fields the ball. He throws the ball. If you want to be a good manager, get good ballplayers."

The Redlegs themselves are the first to quarrel with Birdie's earthy formula. Good players can be the making of a good manager, but Birdie's success is proof enough that a good manager can be the making of good players

One after another, all the Redlegs lavish praise on Birdie. They know what he means when he says, "There ought to be a second-string or junior Hall of Fame for guys like me. I'll read about some superstar who has had a bad season and the writers apologize when they say, 'He only hit .311 that year.' Listen, I had a lifetime average of .270–and I'm proud of it. I poured my life's blood into it. I clawed and scrambled and fought and hustled to get it." Thanks to Birdie, the whole Redleg team is clawing and scrambling and fighting and hustling. They have learned that belligerent approach to baseball from a man who never knew anything else.

[*Author's note:* This piece was reprinted from the July 8, 1957, issue of *Time* magazine. Used with permission.]

1

"There was only one catch and that was Catch-22, which specified that a concern for one's own safety in the face of dangers that were real and immediate was the process of a rational mind."

–Joseph Heller, *Catch-22*

Catch as Catch Can

When I used to give speeches during the winter at one of those Elks Club sports banquets around New England, I usually started out with a joke to warm up the group and to find out whether I was talking to a baseball audience or just plain folks. My big joke went something like this:

"Everybody talks about how difficult it is to be a catcher and how tough the job is and everything else. You wear all that hardware, and it's supposed to be heavy and hot and uncomfortable. The truth of the matter is, being a catcher is easy. You give a sign, you stand up and get ready to catch the ball, and when the ball is hit everybody out in the field has to run somewhere. Any time a baseball is hit there should be movement by every player. Each player should move one step at a time in the direction of the play.

Now the great thing about being a catcher is that he doesn't have to move at all. He doesn't have to do anything. But a smart, old catcher backs up first base when there's two out and the dugout is on the first-base side. He shuffles down to back up first base on an infield ground ball so that if the runner is out, the catcher can just turn to the right and sit down. What could be easier?"

OK. So it isn't very funny, but it usually broke the ice and gave me a sense of who my audience was, and after the ripple of laughter was over I could go on from there and talk about catching. Or if nobody laughed I'd know that it would be better to tell a few stories about something else.

There are things about a catcher most fans don't even think about, but these things are important as to why a sharp catcher is critical to winning a ballgame. First off, the catcher is the field manager. He's the only player who plays with the whole game right in front of him. Take the pitcher. He has his back to everybody except the catcher. And outfielders are looking at the backs of everybody else. The catcher is the only one who plays his position outside the base lines and he's the only one who has personal contact with each opposing player. A guy is in the box and you've got him 2 and 2, and the guy moves his left foot back just a little. An outfielder can't see that. Not even the pitcher is likely to see that. But that little move tells a smart catcher whether the guy is going to pull or go to the opposite field. The catcher sees every pitch and he's in on part of every play. He's the only one who needs special equipment. He's the only player that every other player on the team is facing. And the ballgame doesn't start until the catcher squats and gives the sign.

Calling signs, of course, is one of the most significant things a catcher does; that reminds me of a story I used to tell at those New England banquets. Often they were the same stories I'd heard other players tell, but mine sometimes had different endings. This happened with a tale that Ted Williams used to tell.

Now I love Ted Williams. We played against each other before the war, and after the war we found ourselves teammates on the Red Sox. This one day after a game with Cleveland when Lou Boudreau had hit us pretty good, Ted Williams walked by my locker and said, "You're a nice guy, Birdie, but you're a dumb catcher." I just looked at him, wondering what was coming next. He just kept walking. Now on that afternoon Lou Boudreau hit line drives that had sent Ted Williams chasing all over left field, and Ted must have thought it was my fault for calling the wrong pitches. He brought it up the next day while we were standing by the batting cage and I said, "OK, Ted, if you're so damn smart, you call the pitches." Right there we worked out some signs so that when Boudreau came up to bat I would look out to left field

Ted Williams—my friend and teammate, and one of the greatest ballplayers of all time.

and Ted would signal me. He would put his hands on his hips to signal a fastball, or touch his cap for a curve, or hands on knees for a change-up, something like that.

Now there are two endings to this story: the one Ted Williams tells and the one I tell, which of course is what really happened. What actually happened is that the first two times Boudreau came up, Ted called the pitches and Lou hit two doubles to left, which Ted had to chase into the corner. The third time Lou came up I looked out to Ted to get the sign but he had turned his back on me and was facing the Big Green Monster, I think out of shame. So I walked out toward the mound and yelled, "You lose your nerve, Ted?"

In his ending of the story, he claimed I crossed him up and changed every one of his calls to something else. But I honored our deal, and that's my version of the story, and I'm sticking to it.

Another baseball legend I encountered along the way was Yogi Berra. This was in New York during the 1947 World Series. It was a subway Series, the Yanks against Brooklyn. A World Series is always a baseball industry event, a respite after the season that gives players a chance to catch up with old friends, so I stayed over in New York to watch the games.

It was Yogi's rookie year. He sometimes played outfield and at other times, catcher. This was, of course, his first World Series. In the first game, Jackie Robinson got on base and took a big leadoff, teasing and taunting the pitcher. On the first pitch he took off for second. Yogi's throw was in the dirt and very late, and after that every time a Dodger got on base he made Yogi's life miserable. The press was merciless and called Yogi a clown.

Sixty years later I remember a conversation I had with Yogi following that first game. I remember it because it was the first time we talked. I only knew him as a Yankee and I was playing for somebody else. I found out that Yogi was a real down-to-earth, nice man. Always has been. Very real. Something in baseball that we sometimes lose sight of is the fact that there are great players out there who are real.

After that first game I was walking through the lobby of the Edison Hotel in the Theatre District in New York and Berra came by. As we were passing, he turned and said, "Hey, I want to talk to you."

I said, "OK."

And he said, "You saw what happened out there today. These guys are driving me crazy."

"Hell, yes, I saw it, and it wasn't your fault, Yogi. Your pitchers aren't holding the runners on." I looked at this guy and thought about it. He was what, maybe 12 years younger than I was? You've gotta like this guy. There was something so pure about the way he spoke. I said, "Yogi, before the first pitch tomorrow you'll take the ball and you'll throw it to second base, and you'll make a real good throw to second base, and you'll prove to everybody in the whole goddamn world that the pitcher is the reason that they're stealing the bases. But if you go ahead and you hurry your throw when you really don't have a chance to get the guy anyway, then, Yogi, you're going to be the bum, and there's no reason for that. Make the pitcher hold them on."

And that was the first conversation I ever had with Yogi. The fact that he stopped me and brought it up made me feel pretty good. Later on when he became manager of the Yankees, he wrote me a letter about something or other. I kept it–a nice letter that sounds just the way he talks.

I'm sure Yogi would agree that it's awfully hard for a young catcher to catch a great young pitcher if he has never caught a great old pitcher. In other words, when you're going to catch a rookie Mel Parnell just coming up to the big leagues and you've caught a Lefty Grove, you know from catching the one what the other needs to learn. You know by comparison what one can do and what the other has to master in order to be great. The result is that when you're catching the young pitcher you can steer him into that groove of greatness that otherwise might take him a year or two longer to find. And if the young catcher himself doesn't know his pitcher's potential, then you have two guys battling each other and a lot of talent and time going to waste while the rookie pitcher learns to come into his own–if he ever does!

As a catcher you must understand, and you must make your pitcher understand, that not only is each pitch an important part of each game but also that each pitch is of equal importance. Usually I could keep a pitcher's mind from wandering just by firing the ball back to him as hard as I could. And if that didn't work and we went ball one, ball two, then I would walk out there and say, "Hey, God damn it, give it a little more effort."

The only guy in baseball who gets to know everybody is the catcher. He's the guy who's there when the umpire comes out and when the batter comes out. And when the batter comes up you say, "Hi. Hello. How you doing?" No other ballplayer gets to talk to every other ballplayer. The catcher is closest to every other player, and over time can form many a friendship. It could happen to a first baseman, but a batter would have to hit a lot of singles to make a friend of a first baseman.

2

"That's all I'd do all day. I'd just be the catcher in the rye and all. I know it's crazy, but that's the only thing I'd really like to be."

–J. D. Salinger, *The Catcher in the Rye*

The Nashua Millionaires

My mother always said what a great guy my father was and I had to believe her. But I don't remember him. I was born in Burlington, Vermont, in 1912. He was Charles Tebbetts, a clerk with the Swift meatpacking people, and soon after I arrived he was transferred back to his hometown of Nashua, New Hampshire, where he died. I was only three and never knew him; nor did my older sister, Kathryn, or my brother, Charlie, remember much about him. From how people talked, we came to assume that booze had something to do with his early demise. So there was Ma, alone in Nashua with three little kids and no income.

My mother was named Elizabeth, daughter of James Ryan, whose forebears arrived from County Cork during one of Grover Cleveland's presidencies. Ryan raised a large, healthy, devout brood of Catholics. When each child graduated from high school, they were expected to help provide or get out.

Susan Tebbetts Mitchell on

Life with Birdie

Another time somebody came to the door–and this is why he was special–guys came to the house to fix the furnace. Now remember, we have had this house for 28 years. And he turned around to Mom and said, "Baby, where do we keep the furnace in this house?" He called everybody "Baby." And then Mom would always say, she'd say things like, "You know what, Birdie? You're not participating in the family life. You're never here. I'm not getting up tomorrow. See what it's like to get your ass out of bed tomorrow, and see what it's like to get these kids off to school." We'd get up and Dad would be sitting at the dining room table and he'd say, "All right. We're having a contest. Whoever makes the best pancakes I'm going to give 10 bucks." Next thing you know four kids are in the kitchen whipping up pancakes. "Who do you think makes the best pancakes? Let's take a vote. Fine. Congratulations. Bye. Bye now, out the door. Have a nice day." And he'd give us each a buck.

My Aunt Anna, a gentle, tentative, timid woman, went to work in what they called the "shoe shop," sewing the tongues on the uppers of Thom McAn shoes. She would live as a spinster into her eighties, spending all of her working days there, helping maintain the Ryan home up on Crown Hill. Another of my mother's sisters, my Aunt Eva, just barely 18, clutching a brave heart, a cardboard suitcase, and a high school diploma, boarded a train that carried her to New York City. At Brooklyn Hospital she began training as a nurse. She liked the discipline, order, and visible results of the operating room and found herself working beside a young intern. Soon they were dining together under the gaslights at Gage and Tollner on Fulton Street (it's still there, unchanged, and still a great restaurant), and on Sunday mornings they would promenade across the new Brooklyn Bridge. Once the young doctor's practice in a small town upstate was under way, they married and begot my cousin Jimmy, who is responsible for assembling this book.

There have been lots of accounts of how the nickname "Birdie" came to be, all of them wrong. As the family tells it, my Aunt Hilda peeked into the cradle when I was a little squirt and remarked about the size of the baby's tiny mouth. "Like a bird's," she said, and from that day forward little Georgie's name inside the family was Bird. The "Birdie" corruption came later, and who cares how?

But a nickname is important to any ballplayer. If he becomes a great ballplayer, the nickname somehow allows fans to put themselves on an equal footing with the great one. And the more fans, the more money in the guy's pocket. If he's just a run-of-the-mill ballplayer, the well-chosen nickname somehow confers a wacky kind of affection on a personality that might not otherwise be all that interesting. I'm thinking now of "Ducky" Medwick and my old friend "Schoolboy" Rowe. Rowe's given name was Lynwood. What ballplayer would want to be called Lynwood? See what I mean? A good nickname also gives a ballplayer a certain cachet in newspaper accounts and helps convey some sense of personality off the field, which is important if you are negotiating with tightwad owners for a pay increase.

The Tebbettses were poor. My widowed mother took in wash and sewing and other odd jobs to keep bread on the table. We kids bathed every Saturday night in a big basin set in the middle of the kitchen floor, and every Sunday morning we'd go to Mass at St. John's, then go up to Crown Hill where Grandmother Ryan lived to help shovel sidewalks, mow grass, and haul out the ashes from her huge cast-iron kitchen stove. Our reward was a dime.

Charlie and I did lots of things to earn money. I was custodian in a pool hall, which is where I learned to play pool and eventually got so good I was the player for the house and made good money. Charlie and I also sold sandwiches after school aboard the trains that ran between Nashua and Boston. On Friday nights when Charlie and I would put our earnings on the kitchen table,

Ma would scoop it up and stuff it away somewhere, leaving each of us a quarter.

I ran away a lot. Years later when I was visiting the home of Dizzy Trout, the great Detroit pitcher, we swapped stories about running away from home. A funny thing happened as I was telling Dizzy about escaping from home by walking up the railroad tracks as a tyke. It dawned on me while telling him my stories that I had unconsciously timed my escapes so that I would always happen to run into Uncle Gene O'Leary coming the other way. He was a firefighter and always walked home along the tracks at the end of the day, so when I ran away my survival instincts must have driven me in the direction of Gene. Dizzy and I had a good laugh over that.

There was a playground on Pearl Street right next to the tenement where we lived, and on summer nights after the others had been called home to bed, I was always the last to leave. Nashua was a mill town then. It has since gone high-tech, but back then it was blue-collar. The kids I played with were second-generation Italians, Poles, or, like me, Irish. The Canadian province of Quebec was just a few hours away, and there was a big influx of French Canadians as I was growing up in the twenties. We learned how to get along with each other on the playgrounds long before anyone ever heard of such a thing as ethnic harmony. That stood me in good stead as I moved into the larger world of baseball.

I had no father and not even a memory of one, so I went out and found one. He was Arthur Ryan, Ma's older brother. Arthur was manager of the local semipro baseball team, the Nashua Millionaires. Arthur was a magnificent man. Big, buff, strong, and patient. I attached myself to his team, became its mascot and batboy, and along the way began to learn catching skills from the Millionaires' catcher, a guy named Clyde Sukeforth. Then when I was about 13, or maybe 14 or so, a major league barnstorming tour came to town. There was a lot of excitement in the days before the barnstormers arrived. The star pitcher was going to be the great Lefty Grove, who threw the ball at nearly 100 miles an hour. He was guaranteed $25 for every local batter he struck out. I sat down and figured something out. If he pitched only seven

As batboy for the semipro Nashua Millionaires. The fellow in the middle is a fan, and the guy on the end is the team's manager at that time, Tom Whalen.

innings and struck out everybody, that's $525! Just for working maybe an hour!

When Lefty's team arrived at the ballpark to play the Millionaires, the major leaguers were missing a catcher. After a conference around home plate, Uncle Arthur offered them his nephew, little Georgie Tebbetts. I remember looking up at Lefty Grove's face when he looked down at who his catcher was going to be and saw murder in his eyes. I don't remember what happened after the game got under way, but legend has it that I always dropped the first two strikes and managed to hold on to the third. After the game, Uncle Arthur told me not to tell Ma that I played that day, that she'd kill him if she found out he let me stop Lefty Grove's fastball.

My family would tell that story for the rest of my life. It makes a great story, and most of it I guess is true. If it doesn't explain Arthur it certainly begins to explain me and the beginning of my long journey through the big leagues. Arthur Ryan was the only father I ever knew, and he set me on a course from which I never wavered for the rest of my life.

I loved athletics. In my high school years I was quarterback on the All–New Hampshire high school football team and was good at basketball and, of course, baseball. Even so, things were tough at home. Yet all during those growing-up years there occurred a monthly certainty that brought great comfort to Ma and our family. The first of every month a check would arrive from Aunt Eva's husband, a doctor in a small town in upstate New York. The check covered the rent on our home. The doctor was a mythical figure. Remote, kind. He was revered in our house, but we never saw him.

Meanwhile, I was in demand during summer vacations for an Elks team or firefighter's league team when they needed somebody to put on the pads and take the pitches from local hotshots.

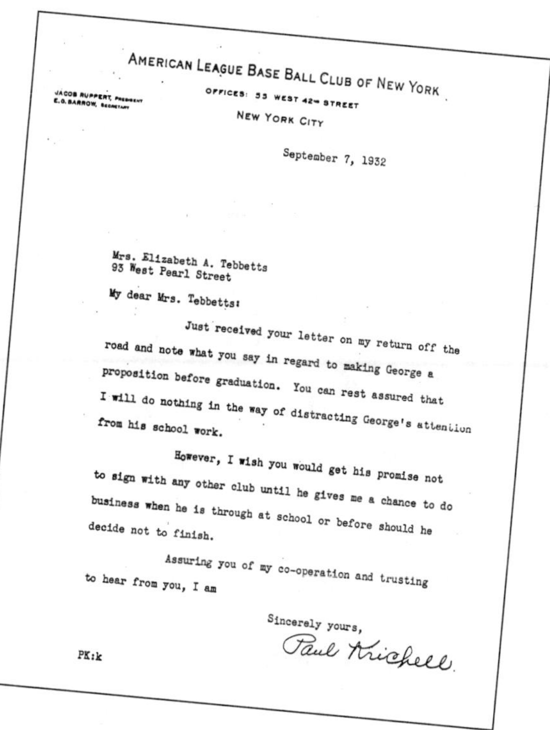

AMERICAN LEAGUE BASE BALL CLUB OF NEW YORK

JACOB RUPPERT, PRESIDENT
E.G. BARROW, SECRETARY

OFFICES: 55 WEST 42ND STREET
NEW YORK CITY

September 7, 1932

Mrs. Elizabeth A. Tebbetts
93 West Pearl Street

My dear Mrs. Tebbetts:

Just received your letter on my return off the road and note what you say in regard to making George a proposition before graduation. You can rest assured that I will do nothing in the way of distracting George's attention from his school work.

However, I wish you would get his promise not to sign with any other club until he gives me a chance to do business when he is through at school or before should he decide not to finish.

Assuring you of my co-operation and trusting to hear from you, I am

Sincerely yours,

Paul Krichell

PK:k

Paul Krichell, the famous scout who signed Lou Gehrig, wrote this letter to my mother on behalf of the Yankees. But it didn't work—the Tigers made a better offer so I signed with Detroit.

By my senior year, 1929–1930, the Great Depression was under way, and I had offers of athletic scholarships to several colleges. Then a guy named Paul Krichell showed up on our doorstep and started talking to Ma. He was a Yankees scout. He was the same guy who had signed Lou Gehrig, and he made an offer to sign me. I've still got his letter to Ma laying around somewhere. But a better offer came from the Detroit Tigers. They gave us a bonus that not only wiped out the family debts but also included four years at the college of my choice. That was the offer that excited my mother. And her sisters. And Uncle Arthur. Meanwhile, my brother, Charlie, continued to support Ma in his grim factory job at the Nashua Coated Paper Company. Charlie was a great guy, and he never was jealous or begrudged me the lucky breaks that came my way. He was best man in my wedding. Charlie died too young.

My agreement with the Detroit ballclub was signed the same year of the stock market crash, and the following fall of 1930 Hoover presided over a nation devastated by the Depression, with men standing in breadlines. Things were so bad then that the former president of our bank was trying to take my job in the pool hall. He could have it.

I set off for Providence College. The sponsor of the Nashua Millionaires ballclub was a guy named Francis Parnell Murphy, who later became governor of New Hampshire. He owned the shoe shop where my Aunt Anna sewed the tongues on Thom McAns, so I got a free pair of two-tone wing-tip bluchers, size 9D. Uncle Frank Ryan bought me a pearl-gray Adams felt fedora, and with Charlie's herringbone single-breasted suit let out here and there, Ma saw me off on the 8:43 for Boston, changing at South Station to the NYNH&H for Providence.

Catching for the Providence College team. An athletic scholarship paid my way.

I was a stocky, muscular kid of 17, standing just under 6'. I had $8 in my pocket to last the whole semester, looked spiffy in my new duds, and was eager to show the world. Scared to death and with good reason.

The college was and is run by Catholic clergymen. For four years the Dominican Fathers of Providence drilled me on the writings of Plato, Aristotle, St. Augustine, and Thomas Aquinas and made me practice elocution and polish my manners. In turn, I gave them good sweat on the basketball court and on the diamond. One Saturday night during this time, I was with the team returning from a basketball game against Fordham in New York. We got as far as Bridgeport in Connecticut when I came down with acute appendicitis and had to undergo emergency surgery in the local hospital.

When I was well enough to travel, my Aunt Eva, who lived just an hour away, drove her Studebaker over to Bridgeport and brought me back to her home in upstate New York to recuperate. And what a home. A big white house on a tree-lined street. I had my own room. There was a live-in cook and a lady who did the cleaning and made the beds and a man who did yard work. My Aunt Eva would see to it that I got breakfast in bed. We had meals in a candle-lit dining room. Aunt Eva and the doctor had just returned from a six-week grand tour of Europe.

That time with Aunt Eva was my first encounter with a tow-headed eight-year-old cousin. He was a fresh kid. He came into my bedroom the first morning and stared at me. To get rid of him I offered to show him the scar of my operation, threw back the bedcovers, pulled back the bandage, and exposed the raw, bloody scab left by the surgeons a week before. That kid never woke me up again. That same fresh brat would someday become the man to urge me to put down these words about a baseball life.

It seems impossible to convey to this generation the way things were in those times. The difference probably can best be described by our music. Our high school music was ragtime and jazz, and in our college years we danced cheek-to-cheek to sentimental ballads and big band swing. It was happy music, innocent. It was a hell of a lot of fun. At college on Saturday nights there was always a dance in some high school gym. A big night on the town was scraping together a dollar to buy two tickets to a movie and holding hands in the balcony, then stopping off for a lemon Coke at a soda fountain on the way home. We smoked cigarettes because it was thought to calm the nerves and aid digestion and because on the backs of magazines advertisements showed big-league ballplayers smoking them. My favorite brand was Old Golds. Fifteen cents a pack.

My romantic interest during my student days was a young gal at a nearby teacher's college. It was a chaste relationship, as most were in those days, and there was an understanding that upon graduation I would become a professional ballplayer, she a teacher, and we would marry and live happily ever after. After graduation I went right to work as a catcher for the nearby New Bedford club in the New England League and took a room in a rooming house.

One Sunday early in the season in New Bedford my girl came out to see me play. She sat in the rickety grandstands, among the cheering, jeering unwashed, among the hawkers of pop and peanuts and Cracker Jack, and she saw the grime and sweat and spit of the game and decided it was not a life she wanted to share. That was the end of that romance, or so I thought.

Two summers later I was catching for Detroit in Boston's Fenway Park when I glanced into the stands and there she was. Instant eye contact with the lady of my student days. But when I looked again, she was gone. I heard later on that she married a mail carrier and had a bunch of kids. The last I heard she weighed 200 pounds.

Down the street from my New Bedford rooming house there was a place called Jimmy Evans Diner, and the ballclub would give us a card with numbers like 10, 15, or 25 on it to represent cents. It was a meal ticket. They were popular during the Depression. You would walk into Jimmy Evans Diner and you would get corned beef and cabbage and a glass of milk for 20 cents. And they would punch out two 10-cent plugs. You ate off that card until there was no more, and then if you were lucky you got another card. But you didn't get any money. The room in which I stayed was paid for by the ballclub, not by me, and I was lucky to get five dollars spending money, but that depended on the gate.

And then the Detroit club had me sent to their Springfield, Illinois, farm club, where I was to get $300 a month. The first payday they called us all together and said, "We'll honor the guys who are married men and the guys with children, and then we'd like to know how much the rest of you guys can get along with until we get our money from Detroit. Meanwhile, we'll pay for your food and hotel." All we needed was $5 or $10 for smokes and candy bars. Anything you wanted to buy was five cents or a dime anyway, and our food was free, so we didn't need much money. Finally, the Springfield club was so desperate for cash to meet their payroll they sold Roy Cullenbine and me to the Beaumont club in Texas, and with the money they got for selling us they were able to pay the Springfield players. It was an exchange between two Detroit farm clubs. The farm clubs were personally owned. I got paid in Texas, but they did not know that whatever I was getting from them was to be matched by Detroit when the season was over.

Beaumont was the site of the first big oil blow-off that turned Texas into the Texas oil capital it is. The oil strike happened in 1901 and was named the Spindletop, and for the next 30 years that single oil field was the biggest oil producer in the world. By the time Roy and I got to Beaumont, it was a boomtown of 50,000 roughnecks and fast women bounded by sandy grassland

and mesquite. July in Beaumont was a sauna run amok; there was enough humidity in the air to choke a shark. Texas had mosquitoes and hungry termites. For culture it had smoky saloons, tent evangelists, and minor league baseball. There must have been a hundred oil derrick skeletons along the skyline at the edge of town, and the heat was augmented by those soaring, searing orange flares on top of the oil rigs. I know one thing. It was a hell of a long way from Nashua, New Hampshire, and even farther from the elm-shaded campus of Providence College.

Roy and I bunked with four other teammates who had rented the second floor of an old house just off Main Street. Those who hadn't won flipping for one of the beds slept on mattresses, old couches, or the floor. But it was cheap. The club owner provided a meal allowance of $1.75, and the first day on the job my expectations ran wild. I ordered up a dinner of soup, steak, fries, salad, pie, and coffee, only to find out that the allowance was a dollar seventy-five per day, not per meal! My pay for the season was $300 a month, most of which I sent back to Ma in Nashua.

I've got to stop here and explain about the word *Ma* and the way we Tebbetts kids pronounced it. We all had New England accents. I didn't find out I had a New England accent until I got to Texas and the guys from the deep south would ask me why I called my mother "Mar." I also learned that I pronounced the word *socks* by saying "sawx," and my word for *soda pop* was "tawnic," and the short word for *automobile* was pronounced "caa," which of course is the way it is supposed to be pronounced. It wasn't until John F. Kennedy was elected president that the world learned we New Englanders had been right all along.

There is a tiresome joke about the man who stops a passerby and asks, "How do I get to Carnegie Hall?" And the stranger answers, "Practice!" That's easy for a fiddle player or a singer. Just close the door, pick up the fiddle, and have at it. But for the athlete whose talent is a team sport, a team is needed to practice and hone the skills. In baseball that means at least 18 men, plus an umpire to keep order.

Minor-league baseball offers nothing more than the opportunity to practice and learn the trade. And for a second-string ballplayer sitting on the bench, it often means a sentence to oblivion. And so it happened that I found myself in this grimy, squalid outpost with a most fragile connection to the Detroit Tigers club, which was about to win its second successive pennant and a World Series.

That's OK. That Detroit team was under the brilliant management of 32-year-old Mickey Cochrane. The problem was that Cochrane was a catcher. The world's best. Cochrane, who would one day enter the Hall of Fame, was at the apex of his career. He had years of useful service ahead of him. The career outlook for the kid from Providence College was bleak, and more than once on the long overnight bus rides between San Antonio, Houston, and Beaumont, I thought about the other guys in my college class, the ones with jobs and mortgages and pregnant wives.

In Beaumont at the time, there was a garage man who was a lover of the game, and as a favor to the guys living in the top floor of the house off Main Street, and in exchange for front-row admission to the games, he loaned us a derelict Essex fresh-air sedan. No top. We took turns driving it. It would sputter along for a few miles, but on occasion it would break down and we would have to abandon it. When we did, we'd tell the garage man where to find it, and he'd tow it back to his garage, get it running again, and give it back to us.

One of my teammates in Beaumont was a great big burly Cherokee Indian named Rudy York, who would someday play a significant role in the emergence of my career. Rudy was slow afoot and his throwing arm had no zip, but when he swung the bat and it connected with the sweet spot, there was a detonation that seemed to vaporize the ball. Rudy's eagle eyes found the sweet spot often enough to alert the Detroit front office. Rudy could neither read nor write. He could tie his shoes and button his trousers (zippers were just then coming in), but he had no sense of how to dress, greet another person, or handle a knife and fork with delicacy in a restaurant. In addition, Rudy was fond of rye whiskey, Camel cigarettes, and fancy women.

One night my friend Rudy and I took the Essex for a joyride and picked up a couple of ladies, Rudy at the wheel and feeling no pain. We ended up amidst the oil derricks outside of town and Rudy asked us, the couple in the back seat, if we wouldn't mind taking a stroll. Get the picture? A flare-lit night, the drunken Cherokee in the open car with a floozy, while the altar boy and bimbo are high-footin' in the oil-soaked sand among the throbbing, bobbing elevators pumping crude.

And then a ruckus broke out in the car with loud cursing and screaming. "I'll take care of that goddamn Indian," said my companion, and with that she broke away, rushed to the car, and changed places with Rudy's girl, who joined me in the shadows. Soon there was heavy breathing, a war hoop, quiet, and a silent ride back to town. Rudy York slept soundly that night.

My second year in the Texas League was well under way, and because I was finally playing baseball every day, my skills were becoming refined. But my impatience and restlessness grew. I was aware that far to the north, the mighty Cochrane was blocking the plate–and my future. But as a right-hander I was learning to bat to the opposite field behind the runner.

When it was clear that Detroit was coming in 19½ games behind the Yankees, Mickey Cochrane brought me up to the big leagues to catch the last 10 games of the 1936 season for Detroit.

I'd arrived. I even popped a home run, and in my first big-league year batted a nifty .303, which I'd never do again.

Now I say that Mickey brought me up to Detroit to catch the last 10 games of the 1936 season. That's what the papers reported, but of course the papers never get it exactly right. Like everything else in life, a lot of what happens is luck. Both good and bad.

3

"Holy Father, do you realize that you and I are both former Cardinals?"

–Ducky Medwick on meeting Pope Pius XII

To the Big Time

Ma kept writing to me in Beaumont all summer long about my tonsils. I'd been having these summer colds and it was interfering with my game, and finally in a letter to Mickey Cochrane asking him about changing my stance, I mentioned about getting my tonsils out. A minor league ballplayer couldn't afford the operation, and I was hoping that somehow the Detroit club could take care of the bill. Nowadays you tell somebody that you're going to have your tonsils out and they look at you like you've got a screw loose. But back then in the 1930s, a tonsillectomy, as it was called, was a very popular medical procedure. I think it was a fad, like everybody today driving these SUVs, because the guy next door has one. Nobody knows why, but I guess in the Depression days surgeons could make good money selling the operation.

So I got back from Waco on a road trip and there was this letter waiting for me from Mickey Cochrane himself. It was about changing my stance and also about my tonsils. He thought taking them out was a good idea too. And so in mid-September,

Some advice—for both on the field and in the doctor's office!—from Mickey Cochrane himself.

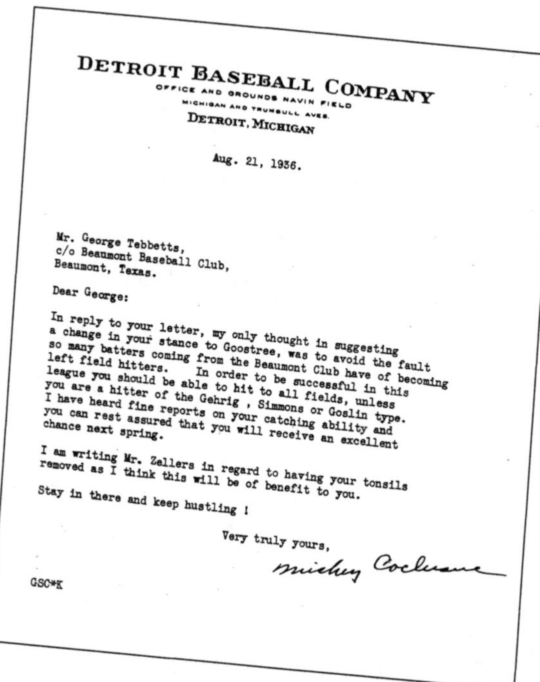

DETROIT BASEBALL COMPANY
OFFICE AND GROUNDS NAVIN FIELD
MICHIGAN AND TRUMBULL AVES.
DETROIT, MICHIGAN

Aug. 21, 1936.

Mr. George Tebbetts,
c/o Beaumont Baseball Club,
Beaumont, Texas.

Dear George:

In reply to your letter, my only thought in suggesting a change in your stance to Goostree, was to avoid the fault so many batters coming from the Beaumont Club have of becoming left field hitters. In order to be successful in this league you should be able to hit to all fields, unless you are a hitter of the Gehrig , Simmons or Goslin type. I have heard fine reports on your catching ability and you can rest assured that you will receive an excellent chance next spring.

I am writing Mr. Zellers in regard to having your tonsils removed as I think this will be of benefit to you.

Stay in there and keep hustling !

Very truly yours,

Mickey Cochrane

GSC*K

after the Texas League shut down and with a couple of weeks to go in the big-league schedule, I took a very, very long train ride to stop off in Detroit for the tonsils before going home to New Hampshire.

I got to Detroit and went to the Detroit clubhouse before getting the tonsil thing done, and Mickey Cochrane asked me to suit up and work out. When I walked out on that field I looked around and, though I didn't know it at the time, there were five future members of the Hall of Fame out there. Now remember, this was 1936 and at that time there was no such thing as the Hall of Fame; that didn't come along until 1939. [*Editor's note:* The first five players were enshrined in the Hall of Fame in 1936, although the museum itself did not open its doors until 1939.] Anyway, the first guy I saw was Hank Greenberg at first base. Then there was

Charlie Gehringer at second and Goose Goslin and Al Simmons in the outfield. Mickey Cochrane was the fifth.

I was at the plate taking infield practice and somebody was hitting fungoes to the outfield, and somehow, I don't know how, I got smacked in the mouth with a ball. I started spitting blood. I went into the clubhouse and rinsed out my mouth, and it was then that Mickey asked me. He must not have noticed that I was bleeding, because he asked if I'd like to catch the game. I said OK.

Elden Auker was the pitcher that day. He was an underhand pitcher and I'd never much caught that kind of a pitch before. And all the while I was learning how to do this, I was swallowing blood the whole nine innings. I remember I got a double and we won the game, and they took six stitches in my mouth when it was all over. So I played 10 games for Detroit in the last three weeks of their 1936 season and had my tonsils taken out at Ford Hospital.

At this point I've got a widowed mother and I am No. 1 in helping support her, and I've got to get a job. Mr. Navin was the general manager, and his right-hand man, a guy named Eagan, said, "What are you going to do this winter?"

I said, "I'm going to have to get a job."

He said, "Well, the Ford Motor Company has a job for everybody that plays for the Detroit ballclub anywhere in the country. So if there's a Ford factory anywhere near where you live, find out." When he saw me the next day he said, "There is a Ford factory in Somerville, Massachusetts, and one in New Jersey. You can work in either one this winter."

Well, Somerville was just about 30 miles from my New Hampshire home, so I took a job in Somerville and took the train down every morning. That's how some of us survived the winters in those days. We had to work.

Most of the Major League owners were not rich men. It wasn't until the millionaire sportsmen like Tom Yawkey and Powel

Crosley came into franchise ownership that baseball began to become an industry. The Connie Macks and the Griffiths who owned the Philadelphia and Washington clubs didn't pay well. They couldn't. Even in New York, Jacob Ruppert, who owned a brewery, didn't pay his Yankee players well. No, sir. He used to negotiate with Red Rolfe, telling him that his salary would be augmented by World Series winnings every year. You had to win it to get that bonus. I made $600 a month my first year up with Detroit. A lot of married guys couldn't make ends meet playing baseball. Some really great players, too.

Too Many Catchers

In 1937 I showed up early, along with the rest of the pitchers and catchers, for spring training in Lakeland, Florida, only to find five catchers vying for a place on the roster. There was the great Mickey Cochrane; Ray Hayworth, a veteran catcher; Cliff Bolton, who'd been around a long time; and Rudy York, who couldn't catch a cold but could hit the ball very, very far and very, very often. Mickey Cochrane tried making a third baseman out of Rudy, figuring he could do less damage at that position. But Rudy couldn't cut it at third, so by Opening Day in Detroit there were still five catchers and only room for two.

I read in a magazine article one time that you could create your own luck if you did certain things and prepared yourself for luck to happen. I had this in the back of my head when Mickey told four of us we were being sent down to the Toledo farm club for more seasoning. He told us this right after infield practice before a game against the Yankees. The other guys showered and dressed for travel, but I figured I'd stay in uniform just in case. The goddamn game went 14 innings, and when Mickey looked down the bench, he saw me and sent me in to pinch hit. I put a double into right field, we won the game, and I was a big leaguer for the next 17 years. Luck is homemade.

Hank

Hank Greenberg broke into the big leagues with Detroit in 1933, and by the time I arrived four years later he was already a superstar, which also made him a very conspicuous Jew. In 1938 he hit 58 home runs, coming within 2 of tying Babe Ruth's 60 homers. But even though he was a star, it did not shield him from anti-Semitic jibes from the grandstands. No, they were brutal. Such were the times.

Greenberg was a kind man. But even he had his limits. Like the time we played the White Sox when somebody from their dugout yelled out, "Greenberg, you're a yellow Jew bastard!" Greenberg let it slide, but then Chicago's Joe Kuhel got on first base and some guys in the White Sox dugout yelled to Joe to draw a throw and spike Hank. And he did. He took a long lead off first and when the throw came in he slid right into Hank's foot and tore a hole in his shoe. Greenberg hauled off and slapped him right in the kisser, and they scuffled and were thrown out of the game.

But it didn't end there. After the game, Hank took off his spikes and walked right into the White Sox clubhouse and said, "Whoever called me a yellow Jew bastard can come right up now and say it to my face." And he looked around the room and finally came to the guy who he knew had said it, but the guy didn't move.

There was nobody in all of baseball who took more abuse than Hank, except Jackie Robinson. But the thing that saved Hank was that at the end of the day he had someplace to go. He had friends, lots of them, in Detroit and in every other city. But Robinson, when he left the ballpark, where could he go? No restaurant would welcome him. He had it rougher than Hank.

One of the first things Hank did for me was to invite me along to a dinner party at Detroit's most elegant restaurant, the London Chop House. The restaurant may still be there on Congress

Street. It was the restaurant where the big-spending vendors of machine tools and paint systems went to schmooze with the engineers and designers from the automobile companies. The owner of the Chop House at that time was a friendly guy, and he seemed to take a liking to Hank's Irish friend, the one who never took a drink. After this dinner party was over, he came up to me, shook my hand, and invited me to come back any time.

"But I could never afford to eat here," I told the man.

The owner's answer was this: "You can come here, sit down, and relax, and we'll hand you a menu. Now, Birdie, it won't be the menu that everybody gets. You don't want that. It will be the help's menu. You will be served the same food the help eats. And you'll pay the same prices they do."

And so I did. I went there a lot, and I always felt welcome. And along the way I became friendly with a young lady who worked at the restaurant greeting and seating customers. She loved dancing and so did I, and on Saturday nights we'd take the trolley up Jefferson Avenue past the Chrysler plant and across the bridge to Belle Isle to a dance pavilion in a city park on a spit of land in the middle of the Detroit River. We'd hop till "Good Night, Ladies" played, then I'd drop her off and trolley back to my Seward Avenue apartment where I'd bed down to be ready for the big Sunday game.

It was the day after one of these dancing Saturday nights that the clubhouse boy told me to go to the office of Spike Briggs. He was the Tigers' general manager, who also happened to be the son of the club's owner, Walter O. Briggs.

On the way up to the office, Hank Greenberg pulled me aside and warned me what was coming, and I began to sweat. He told me that my Saturday night dancing partner was Spike Briggs' mistress. Now, Briggs was also happily married with a growing family. I was expecting the worst and was surprised by Briggs' attitude. He was friendly and cordial, thanked me for my gentlemanly behavior with the lady, and urged me to continue the innocent relationship. Although I kept going to the Chop House, as for the girl, I kind of let that whole thing dissolve.

I'd given up my off-season factory job at Ford. Winters would find me giving talks and making friends on the creamed-chicken-and-peas Lions Clubs circuit around New England for which there would always be a modest honorarium or a wristwatch. I still own a drawer full of wristwatches.

Rudy

Then, of course, there was Rudy York. I roomed with Rudy when we got to the big leagues, and one of my tasks was to be the go-between for Rudy and his wife back in Cartersville, Georgia. Both were illiterate, the York husband and wife, both full-blooded Cherokees, and I was their scribe and reader. I'd write as Rudy would dictate his most intimate feelings to his wife, and she in turn would dictate letters to a writer in Georgia, which I'd read back to Rudy.

I felt sorry for Rudy. Here he is, up in the big leagues traveling to Washington and Cleveland and New York, and he doesn't know how to dress, and he doesn't know how to hold a fork, or order a steak, and he doesn't even know how to hail a cab. Hank Greenberg and I took him under our wing. To start with, Hank took him into a clothing store and got him some decent duds and showed him how to tie a tie.

We got to New York for a three-game series against the Yankees. The Detroit ballclub, and I guess most of the ballclubs, always stayed at the Hotel New Yorker, close to Penn Station at 34th Street and 8th Avenue. I understand that now the Hotel New Yorker is owned by the Moonies, but back then it was a very popular and very lively commercial skyscraper hotel with an air-conditioned lobby and a first-class restaurant, and every room had a radio that didn't work.

Now the reason I'm making such a big thing telling about the Hotel New Yorker is that on a hot summer morning in that air-conditioned lobby, you'd see ballplayers in street clothes lounging around the lobby after breakfast, picking their teeth, having a cigarette, reading about themselves in the morning papers, and chatting with one another, while watching the stylish people come and go. You'd see men in Palm Beach suits and Panama hats wearing two-tone bluchers and women in silk dresses and flowered hats. At the same time, the lobby was where New York reporters would roam about hoping to corner a ballplayer with a good story to tell. Around 10:30 or 11:00 we would all head down into the subway and to the ballpark.

On this one Sunday afternoon in May–it was the 25th of May–in 1937 at Yankee Stadium, Irving Darius Hadley was pitching for the Yankees and Gordon M. Cochrane was at bat when a high inside fastball came out of the white shirts in the bleachers and struck Mickey Cochrane on the skull, rendering a near-fatal blow. A stunned silence swept over the crowd as Mickey was carried off the field.

A great many things happened as a result of that one pitch. These things did not come all at once but over time. Here is a short list. First of all, forever after Irving Darius Hadley became known as "Bump" Hadley. Second of all, it would mark the beginning of the end of Cochrane's playing career. I also think it affected him mentally, but ever so slightly. Third, club owners would eventually close off the center-field bleacher sections to give a good contrasting background for the inside fastball. And 20 years later batters would adopt helmets. Finally, with Cochrane no longer in the lineup, Birdie Tebbetts would divvy the catching chores with Rudy York, meaning I wasn't likely to be soon traded or sent back to the minors. Because, as I say, Rudy couldn't catch a cold, and I certainly couldn't hit 35 home runs. And there is one other thing. That summer of 1937

I began to know that I belonged on a major league baseball club.

It took a while, but by midsummer Mickey returned to managing the Detroit team. Just for a while. And then he left and Del Baker took over.

Detroit's Dilemma

The dilemma facing Detroit was the power of Rudy York's bat and how to get it into the lineup every day without hurting the defense of the ballclub. If there were such a thing as the designated hitter back then, there would be no dilemma. The problem was that the safest place to play Rudy was at first base and that was Hank Greenberg's job. So for my first year up, Rudy and I divvied the catching chores, and the result was that he didn't get to hit enough and I didn't get to catch enough.

But I learned a lot just sitting on the bench near Cochrane. This one day during a ballgame I was sitting there staring off into space and Cochrane said to me, "Watch Gehringer."

I looked over to second base, and as this left-hander stepped into the batter's box, Charlie took three steps back and a half step over. The guy fouled the first pitch and took two outside curveballs. Charlie didn't move. Then the guy hit a line drive foul to left. At that point, Gehringer moved up a half step, and on the next pitch a screaming groundball bounced once and went smack into Charlie's glove. He pulled it in and tossed it to first in one motion. Cochrane looked over to me. I nodded. From then on I started paying closer attention to what Cochrane did and said. And of course that meant I started paying attention to what the pitcher said.

One of the most memorable remarks from a pitcher was before a ballgame when Elden Auker was going to pitch against the Philadelphia Athletics. As he was an underhand pitcher he had a curveball that was a riser instead of a sinker. It was a real teaser to a right-handed hitter. Very effective. And he told me before the ballgame, he said, "Let's not throw any curveballs to Bob Johnson. He zeros in on my curveball."

I said, "OK." So we get into the seventh inning of the ballgame. Bob Johnson is up, and Elden shook off, shook off, shook off, and finally I sat up and said, "Throw what you want." And he threw the slider, and the ball went into left-center field for two bases. The end of that story is that Elden Auker pitched a one-hit shutout and won it 1–0. That pitch cost Elden a no-hitter. This is the story of a guy who knew where he was vulnerable but couldn't resist the temptation.

Here's another example of knowing what your pitcher can do. When I was about to catch Schoolboy Rowe for the first time, Cochrane said to me, "Birdie, don't let this guy go to sleep on you."

I said, "OK."

And he said, "If you call for a fastball and you get a fastball, you know whether you've got that guy's best fastball or not. You're the only one in the ballpark who knows, including him sometimes. So if you call fastball, fastball, and you get two pitches that aren't all out, then you know that either he's lost it or something's wrong."

But with Rowe, it was a case of just being big and lazy. And so Mickey told me, "You go out there and chew him out if he eases up."

He did. We had a two- or three-run lead and he threw a fastball, and he threw another fastball, and I went out there and I said, "Hey . . ." I started to tell him he wasn't trying and he was getting lazy, and when I finished, and this is the truth, he looked at me and he said, "Hey, Birdie. You ain't no Cochrane."

Of course, he was right. But that didn't mean I couldn't learn, and being around great hitters you're bound to pick up things that help you improve. Hank Greenberg pointed out hitting strategies that applied to Bob Feller and the great ones in my day and still apply today to guys like Greg Maddux and Roger Clemens.

(By the way, I always hit pretty well against Feller. That is, until I told that to a reporter during the off-season. The guy printed it and Feller must have read what I said because next time I came up against Feller, in our first game in Cleveland, he threw three straight strikes across the plate and I never once saw the ball.)

As a batter, when you face a pitcher like a Feller or a Clemens, you generally give him everything except one pitch. You walk up there and you hit his fastball and give him his curve. Or if you get into a certain situation where you feel he has to throw the curve, you give him the fastball. You look for one pitch and spot him the other. You do not go up and say, "This is a fastball and the next pitch is going to be a curve." You go up there and spot him the curve. You think to yourself, "If this guy is going to give me a curve, I'm going to give it to him," and then you're cocked for the fastball, and when the curveball comes, it's "Katie, bar the door." There are guys you will hit against where you say to yourself, "I'm going to spot him the curve and hit his fastball, because with two strikes on me I can protect myself against a curveball strikeout and I can't do that against a fastball."

In my opinion there was no sacrifice fly when I played. Sometimes I was in the lineup fifth or sixth, but mostly I was eighth. My job was to get on base and avoid the double play, to make the pitcher make the last out instead of me. I know that if certain rules had been in effect or if I had a contract that said I must hit .290, I might have hit .290. But I wouldn't have been worth doodly squat to the ballclub. I say that predicated on the fact that I hit .270 and that when I hit .270 it helped the ballclub as much as, if not more than, it helped me.

But the main thing about hitting is to never, never get complacent just because you're ahead. Greenberg told me that one time in St. Louis. We were playing the last-place Browns and we were scoring at will. Everybody was getting base hits and having a great time. When the game was over, Hank was sitting by his locker all covered with sweat and madder than a wet hen. We had won and everything had gone well.

I said, "What's the matter, Hank?"

And he said, "I went one for five, that's what's the matter!"

I said, "What the hell is so bad about one for five when we won?"

He said, "Birdie, you've got to go three or four for five against these guys, because when you get up against guys like Lefty Grove and Feller and Ruffing, you're lucky to get even one hit or a base on balls."

And that was his thinking. A good day against a great pitcher could probably be a base on balls. And a good day against a poor pitcher had to be nothing less than two for four. Made sense for Greenberg. I just now looked him up: .313 lifetime batting average. It makes sense for anybody who wants to have a high batting average. That's where the money is.

Baseball Feuds—On and Off the Field

One day my first year up I was taking batting practice when I heard somebody mention that Ty Cobb was visiting in the clubhouse. As a courtesy old ballplayers are always welcome in the clubhouse. And everybody knew Cobb was in there. I'd been hearing stories about Ty Cobb since I was a kid, so when I finished taking my licks I headed in. So did just about everybody else. Everybody wanted to meet this legend, this guy who was maybe the greatest player who ever lived. I waited until he was sort of alone and went up and shook his hand. He chatted with me for a minute and said something nice about what he'd read about me. When I went back out on the field, I looked over toward the dugout and there was Charlie Gehringer just sitting there all alone. I said to Charlie, "Aren't you going to go in and see Cobb?"

And Charlie said, “Not me.”

That’s all he said, and then he looked off into the distance as if he didn’t want to talk about it. Now Charlie Gehringer was the nicest guy in baseball. And Charlie was the only one left on the team who’d played when Cobb was the Detroit player/manager. He had played for Cobb as a rookie, going way back to 1925 and 1926. Cobb was not popular with other ballplayers. After that I never spoke about Cobb again with Charlie Gehringer. I didn’t have to. I knew how Charlie felt.

I had my own conflict with a fellow named Ben Chapman. My second year with Detroit I was catching a game in Fenway Park. Ma and Sis and a lot of old friends and neighbors had come down from Nashua to watch the local kid. To celebrate the occasion Ma baked my favorite lemon pie and sent it in to the clubhouse. Every guy got a little piece. Playing for the Boston Red Sox that day was a fiery outfielder named Ben Chapman, who had recently been traded away from the New York Yankees. He had the same kind of reputation as Ty Cobb, and I know because I’d heard it myself that he was one of the most brutal Jew-baiting tormentors of Greenberg.

So about the middle of the ballgame, on a close play at the plate, when Chapman roared in from third and slammed into me, spikes high, I just blew my stack. I threw off my mask and started throwing punches. Umpires and teammates broke up the melee, and both of us were tossed out of the game, fined, and suspended.

The next morning as I was having breakfast with my mother, sister, and brother in the coffee shop of Boston’s Hotel Kenmore, a couple of players passed by, nodding to me and smiling at my mother. She said, “Good morning.” One guy passed by and said good morning to me and then smiled a big wide smile at my mother and said, “Good morning, Mrs. Tebbetts.”

After he passed, Ma said to me, “Who was that nice man, Bird?”

And I said, "That's Ben Chapman." Ma's jaw dropped, and before she caught herself she slammed down her coffee cup and said, "That son-of-a-bitch!" Sis and Charlie went pale, but I had to laugh.

After that episode, the next stop on the road for the Detroit club was Yankee Stadium. There was a place under the stands near the Yankee dugout where players could gather and grab a smoke before going out on the field, and as we were standing there a bunch of Yankees wandered by. One of them was Lou Gehrig. He stopped, looked us over, and said, "Which one of you is Tebbetts?"

I said, "I am."

He looked at me and said, "Did you land a good punch?"

"Yes, sir."

"Are you still mad?"

"Yes, sir."

"Would you fight him again?"

"Yes, sir."

"Well, if you ever do and you land two good punches, I'll buy you the best suit you will ever own."

And with that, Lou Gehrig turned and climbed the staircase, grabbed a bat, and stepped into the batting cage.

That is a true story, and it's a story about how a friendly relationship developed between a rookie and a baseball great. It also shows a side of Gehrig that has probably never been told before. But the other interesting thing is the offer to buy someone a new suit. You wouldn't think of buying somebody a new suit today. People quit wearing suits. But that was a grand gesture during the Depression of the thirties when the fact that you were wearing a suit told your status. And in those days a new suit came with two pairs of pants.

Chapman isn't the only guy I hold a grudge against from that time. Here it is 60 years later and I still find it hard to forgive Jerry

Priddy. Catchers spend most of their careers crouching down behind the plate and in doing that develop a thickness on the upper thigh. This tends to make most catchers slow on the base paths. So, by God, I had to run like hell to make every base hit I ever got. And this one day in a ballgame I hit a sharp grounder to the second baseman and took off running as fast as I could. When I had gone about 10 steps I looked up and Jerry Priddy was standing in the infield with the ball in his hand, and instead of throwing it to first for the out, he just held it there, looking and laughing like hell while I was trying to run out the play, knowing that the longer he held it, the longer and harder I had to run.

That's a good example of somebody trying to show you up in a way that does damage to the game and damage to a ballplayer's source of income. And it's showing you up in a way that has nothing to do with winning or losing.

The ballpark is not the only place where fights break out. And no wonder. The ballplayer's life, in spite of the fact that he's one of a team, contains the same jealousies, betrayals, alliances, and paranoias as life at a corporation. But there are two very big differences. First of all, everything that is overheard in the clubhouse or dugout has a good chance of appearing in bold headlines in the pages of the newspaper the next day. Besides, you can be sure the reporter that printed the story got it wrong. The other thing is, unlike a guy in a suit at IBM, the ballplayer is usually young and immature and spends half of his working life away from home.

Why do fights break out among guys on the same team? It usually happens when a teammate tries to show you up. On any given day during a game, there is always some kind of subplot going on, one of those invisible, slow-burning grudges that sooner or later has to come to a head.

I remember this one time when Tommy Bridges was pitching. Tommy Bridges was a good friend of mine. I always caught him.

On this one day we started a ballgame in Detroit and it was an important one. On the first pitch of the ballgame I got set and put my fingers down. I put down for a fastball and he shook his head. I didn't think he saw the sign, so I put the fastball down again. But he shook his head. So I put curveball down and he shook his head. So I put change-up down and he shook his head. Now, this is the first pitch of the ballgame! I'm the catcher, and he's already gone through every goddamn pitch he's got. So there's something wrong here. So I walked out in front and I said, "You OK?"

And he snarled, "Yeah!"

So I said, "Hey. Let me tell you something. I'll catch this goddamn ballgame without giving you a sign. Anybody can catch that shit you throw up." I was mad. And everybody on the bench knew it. I went back to home plate and set up. And he kept looking at me. And I said, "Throw the goddamn ball."

Now here was a guy with the best curveball in the history of baseball, and I had been catching him in every game he pitched. I always said I could hit any pitcher I ever caught, and I could. Because I knew exactly what they were thinking. So here we go into about the sixth inning, and Bridges is trying. Pitching hard, throwing like hell, and I'm just catching–the fastball, the curve, the change-up, and the slider. And I never call a single pitch. I don't know it, but they know on the bench that I'm mad, and they know what we're doing.

So we get into the sixth, and we've got a situation like it's 3 balls and 2 strikes on a guy, where you either got to make him swing or walk him. And so I'm sure he's going to throw the high fastball strike, and he throws a ball. I reach up to grab it and it hits me on the toe! I'm down in the dirt in pain holding my toe and Tommy, up on the mound, throws his glove up in the sky, laughing, and the bench guys are laughing, and Tommy looks down and says, "You all right?"

I say, "Yeah."

And he says, “Well, you better start giving me signs.” And whatever the grudge was, we quickly got over it.

As I tell this story, I think about all of that silly showboating and gloating and prancing like a ballet dancer that you see watching pro football on TV when a receiver scores a touchdown. You’d think that the guy scored all by himself and that there weren’t 10 other guys clearing a path for him. You never, never see that horseshit in baseball. I can’t imagine a guy like McGwire, after he’s hit one out of the park, prancing around home plate trying to show up the pitcher. In baseball, if you’re lucky, you take your high fives from your team and maybe tip your hat if the crowd is cheering, and then hide in the dugout, knowing that the next time up you may strike out with the bases loaded.

The Golden Age

The thirties were a golden moment in baseball. This was in spite of the Depression, in spite of the ethnic and racial meanness, and in spite of the grim future with war storms brewing overseas. Baseball really was the national pastime. It had no competition. Moreover (and this will sound strange to a generation brought up on television), with Red Barber or Mel Allen doing the play-by-play, you could actually watch a ballgame on the radio. By God, it was damn near visible. Pro football was no more exciting on radio than college football and didn’t have a loyal audience out there. It was once a week, and few people had ever really played sandlot football, so it was left to the masochists who were willing to pay good money to sit in grandstands on Sunday afternoons shivering in the snow. Basketball was only a high school sport that ended senior year. Hockey was fast, but the Canadians had barely spilled over into the smoky arenas of four northern cities. Moreover, a hockey game required advanced technology and ladies were not welcome.

So baseball had everybody’s attention. During the day, radios would broadcast the play-by-play of local games, and the broadcast would be picked up on little sets in saloons, cow barns, machine shops, gas stations, and grocery stores. A guy could milk a cow, fill a prescription, pump gas, run a drill press, or change a clutch and all the while picture in his head the men in white flannels romping on the green grass between the chalk lines. In the thirties, most everybody was poor or struggling and eager for heroes, and these guys were the only superathletes that were visible: DiMaggio, Greenberg, Gehrig, Gehringer, Feller, Williams, Boudreau. The word that was used to describe them was *class.*

1939

So much happened in 1939. On May 2 in Detroit we were about to start a game against the Yankees when an ominous murmur began along the bench that soon swept through the ballpark. When the Yankee manager, Joe McCarthy, went to the plate to give the umpire the lineup card, Lou Gehrig was not on it. He had taken himself out of the lineup. What was going on? Gehrig hadn't missed a game in 15 years. Lou went straight from the ballpark to the Mayo Clinic, where he was diagnosed with a fatal disease, which soon came to bear his name.

It was the year that the king and queen of England came to America on a goodwill tour and to visit "The World of Tomorrow," the gigantic New York World's Fair.

By then I had become a good catcher. Really good. Not by way of great natural ability but by hard work and concentration. And also because of one other factor that people don't often think of when they evaluate a ballplayer, and that is that when you play with and against great ballplayers you absolutely must play the very best you can play or you will soon find yourself out of a job. Playing with great players doesn't make you a great player, but it makes you play as well as you possibly can. And my superior catching skills made me the obvious choice over York behind the plate. I played in 100 games in the 1939 season.

Del Baker played Rudy at first base for 19 games–when Greenberg had days off–and the rest of the time he would catch. But Baker still had trouble getting Rudy's bat into the lineup every day.

We were headed for a bleak finish, and on the train after losing three straight to the last-place St. Louis Browns the team morale was at an all-time low. I forget what happened at the ballpark that set Rudy to brooding, but he did brood. Somberly. Then he began to take on bourbon and brood some more and talk loud and angry. Finally he got up and headed out of the dining car yelling that he "was going to get that no-good son-of-a-bitch Baker."

Now word got to our manager, Del Baker, that Rudy was looking for him. So Baker, who wasn't the most inspiring leader, barricaded himself in his bedroom. (Only the manager rated a bedroom in the Pullman car; the rest of us slept in berths.) Rudy beat on Baker's door, yelling his head off until the conductor and some of the rest of us got him to quiet down by threatening to stop the train at the next station and call the cops.

As the season came to an end, Hitler invaded Poland and World War II was under way. But that war was way over in Europe. In this country we were caught up in our own busy lives, and we tried to put the war out of our minds. There is no doubt that the country wanted very badly to stay out of it.

The year 1939 was important to me for another reason. It was the year that Detroit acquired a hot young pitcher from the Pacific Coast League's team in Seattle. They paid a lot of money for him, and as I remember, in those days if you paid more than such and such amount of money for a player you had to put him on the team roster. You couldn't farm him out to the minors until a certain amount of time had passed. This kid, Fred Hutchinson, had won 25 and lost 7 the year before in Seattle. And he could hit. He was 19, a rugged kid, handsome, well mannered. He looked like a movie star. And he threw like hell. His first time out in Detroit they shelled him without mercy. So after the predetermined amount of time he was sent down to the minors, but he came back a few months later. I liked Fred Hutchinson. I was seven years older. I called him "Hutch" and decided I would help him the way Greenberg had helped me and do whatever I could to

Susan Tebbetts Mitchell on

Birdie's Best Friend

It was Fred Hutchinson who found Anna Maria Island. There was no rhyme or reason for us to be in Anna Maria, except for the Hutchinsons and the Torgesons.

I really do not know why we moved to Florida. But what they told us was, they were moving to Florida for us to have a more normal life than we had in Milwaukee. I think what really happened was Dad's friends started to move to Florida. Florida is hopping in the winter, and when baseball season ends and you're in Milwaukee in the winter, you're freezing. But if you're in Florida, you're golfing with all your friends. So Fred Hutchinson moved to the island and Dad loved it. And then the Pirates trained in Bradenton, and it was always a little hopping baseball area. And at the time Mickey Mantle was there during spring training, along with a lot of the ballplayers and their families. I used to baby-sit for Mickey Mantle. One night I came home with $50, and Dad said, "What the hell are you doing with $50?" And I said, "Mickey Mantle, he won. He told me if he won at the racetrack, he would give me part of his winnings. He gave me $50." Dad said, "Bring it back! You're not worth $50!" I started to protest but he said, "Bring it back! You're not going to take $50 from a ballplayer. He was giving you $50 because you're my kid. You're going to bring it back!" So the next day I had to go back and tell Mickey, "I can't take $50. I can only charge three dollars an hour." And he said, "All right." And Mickey handed me the three bucks an hour.

But the most vivid picture I have of Dad in those days is of Dad and Fred Hutchinson, both in straw hats. These two big guys jammed into Dad's little Fiat heading off to the golf course. Dad always drove thousand-dollar junkers.

help him become a 20-game winner. The reason I thought he could make it was that Hutch had an intensity about him. He was competitive as hell. He had a narrow-beamed focus on winning.

As for our ballclub, we ended in fifth place. Somebody had to figure out a strategy so we'd be in contention the next year. I'd taken a job as a kind of goodwill sports director of a small town in northern Michigan that wanted to be the next Lake Placid. But before leaving for the winter Hank Greenberg and I had dinner at the Chop House, and he gave me some advice that served me well for the rest of my career. He said, "Right before Christmas they're going to mail you a contract for next season. Don't sign it. Don't mail it back. Put it in your pocket and take the next train to Detroit and negotiate with those guys face-to-face. They'll call you a bum and tell you you're no good, and they'll say your batting average is down, and they'll threaten to bring up some kid from Toledo. But you know better than they do what you've done for the team. You're one of the best, Birdie. Make them come around." That Greenberg was a great guy.

Hank took his own advice and when he went out to Detroit to negotiate his contract, he found out that the club had decided to make him change from first base to left field so that they could play Rudy York at first base as the only safe way to get his big bat into the lineup. Hank made them pay a big bonus for making the switch, and I don't blame him. He had been a big star at first base and was taking a gamble on his career by changing to the outfield with the chance that he would look bad out there. But he didn't. After a while he fitted himself right in, and by September we were tied with Cleveland for the pennant.

4

"Yes I'd take my chance with fame,
Calmly let it go at that,
With the right to sign my name,
Under 'Casey at the Bat.'"

–Grantland Rice

The Drive to Glory

I forget where my ballclub opened the 1940 season, but I sure do remember where Cleveland opened. It was at Comiskey Park against the White Sox, and Bob Feller pitched a no-hitter. He was 21 years old. Feller won 27 games that year and struck out 261. If we were going to win a pennant, we had to beat Feller and we had to beat Cleveland. At least that was the way it looked at the start of the season, because they were a great ballclub with great pitching.

But that ballclub would soon be made to beat itself. It's too long of a story to tell here in detail, but what happened was that a bunch of players mutinied against their manager, Ossie Vitt. I read in the papers the things he said about his players, and these were guys I knew and knew how good they were, and I couldn't believe what I was reading. I just knew I couldn't play my best for a guy who would disparage his players to the press the way Vitt did. So these mutineers, including Bob Feller, took their complaint to the Cleveland owner, Alva Bradley, and he backed Vitt 100 percent. Of course, this story broke in the papers, and the writers jumped on it and began calling the Cleveland ballclub the Crybabies.

It was ugly when Cleveland came to Detroit because when their players ran out on the field, the fans started booing and throwing out diapers, nipples, milk bottles, and baby food.

So Cleveland had Feller, but we had Greenberg in the outfield and Rudy York on first. Together they hit 74 home runs. Best of all, our pitchers had a helluva year. Bobo Newsom won 21 games, and Schoolboy Rowe made a great comeback and won 16.

Bobo was a brilliant pitcher. He was big and buff and strong, and you'd know him from afar because his head was narrow like a briefcase, and he had close-set eyes that squinted at you. You'd catch his fastball and it stung. He had a sharp curveball he could put anywhere.

Now, I said he was a brilliant pitcher, which was true, but Bobo was also a whiner. "Oh, Birdie. I got such a terrible hangover."

Throwing for a heads-up double play against the Washington Senators.

"Oh, Birdie, my back is killing me." "Oh, Birdie, I got a letter from my wife and I'm fearful something terrible is going on back home." He was from the hill country of South Carolina, and for some reason he was always begging for sympathy. I found out that if you fell for one of his sob stories his pitching was lousy, so I always brought him up short. Then he'd get mad and throw like hell.

The Cleveland ballclub was playing great baseball throughout the season in spite of their morale problems, and we were trailing them most of the time. But then in the stretch we pulled ahead, and when we went to play the last three games against them, we were leading by two. That meant that to win the pennant we had to win only one out of three. In the first game they were going to pitch Feller, so our manager, Del Baker, decided why waste one of our best pitchers against a guy who's probably going to beat us. He looked around and for that one good reason decided to pitch a kid who'd just come up from our minor league club. The kid was named Floyd Giebell, and in Buffalo he'd just won 15 and lost 17.

So the kid took the mound. But the mood of the Cleveland fans in the stands that day was ugly. I was sitting in the bullpen for the game, and in the first inning when Roy Weatherly hit a fly ball and Greenberg circled to field it, the fans showered Greenberg with a barrage of rotten fruit and tomatoes. It got so bad that umpire Bill Summers grabbed the public address microphone and announced that, unless the disturbance ceased, any Cleveland batter who hit an outfield fly would be declared automatically out.

Things quieted down for a while and from out in the bullpen I watched Giebell pitch in and out of trouble. Then *boom*! I saw stars and the lights went out. When I came to, Schoolboy Rowe looked down at me lying on the ground and told me that somebody in the upper deck had dropped a basket of beer bottles on my head. It had been intended for him. And it ended up in a lawsuit against me! The cops caught the Cleveland fan who dropped it, and when I caught up with him I popped him one, and he later sued.

But Floyd Giebell shut out the great Bob Feller and the Cleveland ballclub, and we won the day and the pennant. Detroit went crazy. And although I was a little dizzy, when I read the story of the game the next day, I took a little satisfaction that Ben Chapman, who'd been traded from the Red Sox to Cleveland, had struck out three times and left six guys on base. That made Ma very happy.

As for Floyd Giebell, now there's a baseball story for you. He beat Feller and won the pennant and never won another big-league game.

* * * * *

A World Series is always a colorful event, and being in the middle of it was exciting and memorable. It gave people around the country a moment to forget that the Nazis were in Paris and that every night London was ablaze and under a rain of German bombs.

Most of the ballplayers invited their families to come in for the big event, and I brought Ma, Sis and Aunt Anna in from New Hampshire and put them up in our big hotel in Cincinnati. Bobo Newsom pitched the first game and beat the Reds 7–2. The excitement was too much for Bobo's father. He suffered a fatal heart attack in the lobby of the hotel, which cast a dark, if unspoken, shadow over our club. Ma spent many hours in the days that followed trying to comfort Bobo. We had run out of pitchers, and in the last game he tried to win having had just one day's rest. As hard as he threw, he didn't have it. We lost in the best of six, and it was heartbreaking. Bobo did his darnedest in spite of his personal tragedy. Almost 60 years later I'm still mad at myself for going 0 for 11 in the Series.

One night during the Series I took Ma, Aunt Anna, Sis, Uncle Frank, and Charlie out to a nightclub. They had never been in a nightclub before, and this was a special occasion because the featured attraction that night was a crooner Aunt Anna adored. She used to listen on the radio to this guy Tony Martin. She was unmarried and had spent her entire life working in a factory and maintaining a home for her parents and later for her bachelor brother, Frank, and her old-maid sisters. I loved Aunt Anna. And she loved Tony Martin. So in this nightclub, when the lights came up after Tony Martin finished his act, on the sly I scratched out a note for Tony and handed it to a waiter.

George Tebbetts Jr. on

Life with Birdie

Pop had a way sometimes of putting his foot in his mouth. When I was in high school he came to a game as a scout. He was with my mom, sitting in front of the mother and father of the pitcher from the opposite team. The father was a preacher. And so they were sitting in the stands, and the kid was pitching. Mom was talking to the kid's parents during the game, but Birdie was just writing notes and stuff, unaware of who was behind him, and finally the preacher said, "Mr. Tebbetts, what do you think of the pitcher?"

And my dad said, "You know what? He's pretty good, but his old man's a goddamn preacher so the poor kid will never make it."

Then the reverend said, "I don't understand."

And Pop said, "Well, you know, a preacher's kid gets into Double A and wins, then loses four in a row and says to himself, 'What the hell, it must be God's will,' and quits trying. That kind of crap takes the fight out of them."

And as he was talking they yanked the kid from the game, and the kid got so mad he threw his glove all the way to the dugout. And Pop said, "That's a good sign! That's a good sign!"

I invited him to stop by our table and please pay special attention to Miss Ryan. I signed it "Birdie Tebbetts of the Detroit Tigers." Favors of this kind are common among people in the entertainment business as long as they are not abused. And Tony Martin, wherever you are, you will never know how much your five minutes of attention meant to our saintly Aunt Anna. She spoke sweetly of you till her dying day.

After the games were over the ballplayers picked up their Series checks and headed in separate directions. With his winnings in his pocket, Rudy York lit out for his farm in rural Georgia, stopping off in town just long enough to pay spot cash for a brand-new two-tone four-door Buick Roadmaster. I guess Rudy got overexcited, because before he drove home he made one more stop to show off his car to a neighbor. The guy saw Rudy's fistful of cash and led him to a pen to show him a lovely sow porker to mate with Rudy's lonely boar. I heard later that Mrs. York didn't appreciate it when she watched the muddy sow hop out of the backseat of Rudy's new Roadmaster.

Dizzy Trout

The American League champions of 1940 slipped into fifth place the following year. I had become very friendly with one of our pitchers who everybody called Dizzy, after Dizzy Dean. But he wasn't crazy. He was very rough, very crude. But he wasn't dizzy, although he was known as Dizzy Trout.

Paul Trout never knew his father, and his mother, whoever she was, turned him out on the streets when he was about 12. He lived in back alleys and under bridges, in boxcars and hobo towns for his early years. A street kid from Texas. Our careers were parallel. Dizzy was single and I was single, but we were different kinds of people. Dizzy liked fine suits and knobby, two-tone wing-tip shoes, loud ties and snappy hats. His favorite was a creamy Panama straw. He was a nice man.

Susan Tebbetts Mitchell on

Life with Birdie

I called him one time when he was scouting for the Yankees and told him, "I met the guy I'm going to marry." And he said, "I'll be right out. Meet me at the L.A. Biltmore. And bring that guy."

Whenever Trout won a home game in Detroit, a great big chocolate cake would mysteriously come into the clubhouse. It was always big enough for everybody to have a piece. Everybody knew that some young girl out there was really crazy about Dizzy. Nobody knew who this secret lady was, and neither did he, and as the season wore on, everybody kept wondering. Then one day Trout came in and said, "I'm going to meet the girl who bakes the cakes tonight. Her parents invited me out to the house."

And the next day, "How did it go, Diz? What did she look like?"

"I met the girl I'm going to marry!"

"The girl who cooks the cake?"

"No. Her sister."

I imagine it involved a lot of dates and a lot of time spent at her house before he finally went to the girl's parents and said, "I'm going to marry your daughter. Then I'm going to build a house. And you're going to come live with us, and you are going to be my mother and father. The mother and father I never had. You're not going to lose a daughter; you're going to get me." And Dizzy Trout did just that. He got married. Built a house. They moved in. He had kids.

All the while, the possibility of the draft loomed large for all of us, including Dizzy. Trout's draft number kept coming up, but for whatever reason, he didn't go into the army. Maybe because of his family and the kids. More likely it was because of his hearing. Anyway, he kept getting turned down once he'd take the physical. This is how he'd tell the story: "I went down to have a physical again last week. They put me through this chamber.

They rang bells and they played music. And they put earphones on me and I went through the whole thing, and then all of a sudden there was a guy behind me and he whispered very softly, 'You can leave now, Mr. Trout.' When he said that I thought, 'That son-of-a-bitch thinks I was going to start walking out the door! Hell no.' I just stood there, like I never heard a word he said. I didn't move and, by God! They turned me down again." Well, that was not the truth, but it was a helluva story. He loved to tell it to anybody who would listen and everybody would laugh like hell.

Before the War

This was the time when DiMaggio was having his 56-game hitting streak. People forget two things about that event. Number one, it was ended in a game against Cleveland with great plays by Lou Boudreau and Ken Keltner. And number two, after that game DiMaggio went on to hit in the next 16 straight.

You look at Joe's numbers and you realize how great he was, because he seldom struck out compared with other great hitters. Look at Reggie Jackson's strikeouts and you'll see what I mean. Joe played 1,736 games and only struck out 369 times. Reggie played 2,820 games and went down swinging 2,597 times.

We'd have these dog days back then that made it hard to want to keep winning. Playing in the sweltering heat in St. Louis or Washington with 30,000 empty seats for a crowd of less than 2,000. It's a wonder some of those franchises survived. One thing that seemed to help was when Connie Mack, who owned the Philadelphia A's, would call up Walter O. Briggs, who owned the Detroit franchise, and with a Sunday afternoon ballgame coming up in Philly ask him to pitch Bobo Newsom to help draw a crowd. Mr. Mack badly needed those ticket sales.

The last Series before the war was between the Yankees and Brooklyn, and the most memorable thing for me about that Series was when Brooklyn's catcher, Mickey Owen, let that third strike get by him and Tommy Henrich took first. The Yankees went on to win. My heart went out to Owen, then and now. He will forever be remembered for that low outside fastball that got away. He was a great catcher.

Hank Greenberg had told me that in baseball the legs are the first things to go. "You've got to get your legs in shape before you go to spring training, Birdie," he used to say. "You want to arrive in camp with a spring in your feet." I took Hank's advice, and soon after New Year's I would take the train to Hot Springs, Arkansas, and get myself in shape. It was a wonderful place to be. Nobody bothered me. The weather was balmy, and after a morning in the gym I'd always find a foursome among some other ballplayers and we'd play 18 holes of golf and hit the hay early.

5

"Good-bye, mama,
I'm off to Yokohama."

–J. Fred Coots

The Day the World Changed

I first heard the news when I was passing by a radio in the lobby of the little hotel in Grayling, Michigan, where I was living that winter. Like everybody else in the country, the first thing I tried to do was figure out where the hell Pearl Harbor was, and then call Ma back in Nashua to try to calm her fears. It took four hours to get through on the phone. She'd been through this before. I had been named for George Ryan, her brother, who'd gone off to the first World War and never came back. So Ma said to me, "You go on with your life. When your country wants you, it will call you."

She was right. It would take time to call up and outfit and train 15 million men, and meanwhile I had to figure out where I fit into this situation. The peace-time army was sort of a joke. The uniforms were shoddy. The guys didn't have rifles, so they drilled carrying broomsticks, and they practiced maneuvers using stove pipes for cannons and dump trucks for tanks. Nobody wanted to give up civilian life for the army and would do most anything to avoid it. But I told Ma before I hung up, "I'm telling you this, Ma. If I hear one gibe from the grandstands about being a draft dodger, I'm going to walk off the field and sign up."

The big question for baseball was what would become of the games during wartime. It appeared to be a needless extravagance what with young men dying on the beaches in the Pacific and women giving up their home life to work in defense factories. President Roosevelt took care of that by proclaiming that baseball should be continued through the emergency as a boost to national morale. Hooray!

The first in our club to enter the service was Charlie Gehringer. He was 39 and didn't have to, but he did. Volunteered. Became a naval officer. That's Charlie Gehringer for you.

Before the war ever started, Hank Greenberg had gotten off the boat after a vacation in Hawaii and was told he'd been drafted into the army! It was still peacetime and the draft was a brand-new thing in 1941, part of President Roosevelt's military buildup. Every young man had to register. I did, along with the rest of the young men in the country. But the war was an ocean away, and it wasn't our war, and day to day we tried not to think about Hitler. Japan was not ever in our thoughts. But here it was. The draft got Hank, and he had to swap his $55,000 salary for $21 a month. What kind of season we would have without Hank was something to ponder.

So the season got underway and one day I got word from the front office that a group up in Flint, Michigan, wanted me to help raise money selling war bonds. During the war the government promoted the sale of these bonds to keep down inflation and raise money for the war effort. You could buy a bond for $18.75 and give it to somebody as a gift. The idea was that buying a bond was supposed to make you feel good. Anyway, if you waited 10 years it could be cashed out for $25.

Bond-selling rallies were held across the country and were usually fronted by movie stars to draw a crowd. Joe Louis, who was World Heavyweight Champion and lived in Detroit at the time, was going to help out. The Tigers front office told me about it and I thought that the least I could do was show up and try like hell to get people to buy bonds. Little did I know what I was showing up for.

The folks running the rally were a young Flint couple. He was a doctor and his wife was very active in civic affairs. During the rally I happened to mention that if these folks were ever in Detroit and would like tickets to Tigers games to please give me a call. Within a week after the Flint rally I got a call from the lady saying she and another woman would be in Detroit on such and such a day and they would like to see a game. I left a pair of box seats at the press gate for them, and sure enough, when I went out for infield practice there she was with her friend, sitting in a field box beside our dugout.

Without thinking too much about it, I went by and said something about joining them for coffee after the game and they said "OK." When I showed up, the lady's girlfriend was not with her. She had to hurry back to Flint. So the doctor's wife and I chatted until there was nothing more to say, and then she said she would like to see my apartment. I took her to my place, a one-bedroom apartment on Seward Avenue, and she settled in and spent the night. I couldn't figure it out, wondering about her husband back in Flint.

The next day she went away, and a week or so later she called saying she was going to be in Detroit and could we get together, and I thought, "Whoa! What am I getting into here?" Just about that time her husband came on the line, and he said, "Birdie, this is so-and-so, and I just want to tell you that we admire you very much and we like you, and I'm grateful to you for being so kind and thoughtful to my wife. I love her very much, but, you see, I'm impotent. And I'm grateful for the attention you are paying to her." I said some nice things to him, that I hoped to see them at the ballpark whenever they wanted tickets and so forth, but that I would not be able to continue the friendship, much as I wanted to. Ballplayers run into many strange situations, but this one sticks in my mind for some reason.

The reports from the battlefronts were alarming. It was horrible. The Americans were being beaten in the Pacific, and ships in convoys in the Atlantic were being sunk by the hundreds by Nazi subs. The further along the season ran, the more I realized I had to do something. Then in midsummer, while we were playing a three-game series in St. Louis, this Army Air Corps colonel left a note at the hotel asking if we could talk over coffee after the game.

Now this guy was stationed at an Army Air Corps base in Waco, Texas, and said he was in charge of morale at the base, in charge of special services. He said, "Birdie, I've got a problem. As a matter of fact, the army has a problem. We've got maybe a million servicemen stationed around the state of Texas, and they're young and away from home for the first time. They are training like hell, and they are lonely, and we can't keep them on base all the time, but when they are off base there isn't much for them to do except get into trouble."

I said, "What are you getting at, Colonel?"

He said, "Birdie, you are probably going to be drafted before the season is over."

I said, "That's right. Any day now."

He said, "If they draft you, you can be sent into the navy or infantry or wherever they need a warm body. You won't have anything to say about it."

I said, "That's right."

He said, "If you let me sign you up now as a buck private with the Army Air Corps, you will go into basic training just like any other recruit, and then you will be sent to officer's training school in Miami. You will graduate as a second lieutenant and be assigned to me at the Waco Army Air Corps base. Then I will send you around the country to sign up major league ballplayers for the Army Air Corps. Friends of yours. As many as you can. Now these ballplayers will go through basic training just as you did and will be assigned to Waco and will have all the duties and responsibilities of the regular soldiers. They will clean latrines, pull KP and guard duty, and be company clerks and supply sergeants and all the rest. But in off-hours they will form a baseball team, which you will manage. You'll play ball against other teams around Texas as a diversion for the thousands of troops stationed throughout the region."

In the Army Now

The first guy I signed up for the air corps was Sid Hudson, the great pitcher of the Washington Senators. Then I got Joe Gordon of the Yankees, and before I was through we had a pretty good major league ballclub. We beat everybody in Texas. Along the way somebody asked me, "Birdie, you must have been great playing against all those semipro clubs and those amateur army teams. You must have batted .500."

And I said, "I stunk."

And that was true. If you want to play great baseball, you must play against great players. We had a helluva team. At one time or another, we had Sid, of course, and Tex Hughson, Max West, Billy Hitchcock, Joe Gordon, Enos Slaughter, Walt Judnich, Howie Pollett, Ferris Fain, Charlie Silvera–I can't remember them all. Good soldiers first, but in time off we played ball. Guys would be transferred and come and go, but I think we were very useful giving all those Texas troops something to do when they weren't training.

Then one day I got a call from some guy in the Pentagon. Some big shot. "Captain Tebbetts? This is Major So-and-So at the Pentagon. We are organizing an army baseball team here in

Washington, and we are ordering the transfer of Corporal Sid Hudson from Waco to Bolling Field here in Washington so he can pitch for our team. I want you to cut orders for his release immediately."

I said, "Major, do you realize what that would do to this kid Hudson? He was a star on the Washington Senators, and now he's in the army, and you want to bring Sid back to Washington to play baseball in front of all those people back there who have their own kids overseas fighting and dying? Major, I'm going to do everything I can to block it."

And he said, "Tebbetts, if you try that and you succeed, I will remember. And you can be sure we will meet again." And he hung up and that was that. And he couldn't do anything about it because I stalled, and within months we were all in the South Pacific.

The Most Important Game

A month or so after D-Day in Europe, the marines took back the island of Guam in the Pacific. It surrendered after 5,000 Japanese tried a suicide attack and 3,200 Japanese died. When things quieted down I was put in charge of morale for a unit of the South Pacific command based right there on Guam. I organized football and baseball teams, and right after the marines took over those islands throughout the South Pacific, we went in and laid out a diamond and a football field and fixed things up so we could play a ballgame for those guys.

One afternoon I was Officer of the Day and going about the routine, inspecting the guys on guard duty. As I was going about the business, I got a call ordering me to see this general. He said, "Are your boys ready to travel if you have to travel?"

And I said, "We can go any time and anywhere you want."

He replied, "I'm putting you on 24-hour alert. I want you to have control of your players at all times and be sure you are able to round them up within an hour."

.is guy said to me, "Are you telling me somebody's going .ırt from a goddamn baseball after what these guys have ·ough?"

ıt up and we played. Everybody yelled like hell and had time. When the game was over, the guys began to dis- twos and threes in their jeeps and tanks. And as I was ny gear together and wondering where I could get under r, this marine colonel came up to me. He was nervous, I ·ll. Hesitant, he said, "How long are you scheduled in ?"

I said, "Two or three days I guess. I don't know."

he said, "Goddamn, Captain. This is the best thing that ›pened." Then he added, "This ballgame was a lifesaver. ıys would have gone crazy without something like this to ır minds off what happened here."

.tood there for a while trying to think of what else to say. ed to walk away and I just looked at him. And then he dead in his tracks, turned around and stared at me for a He raised his hand slowly and threw me a salute and said, the most important game you'll ever play, Captain ." He walked away before I could return his salute.

s later Joe Gordon slid home in a tight game I was catch- he Red Sox. He slid in hard, kicked the ball out of my tood up, dusted himself off, tipped his hat, and said, Captain," before trotting off to his dugout.

d Out and Home Again

Guam I was just walking out of the mess hall when this came running up to me. I forget the kid's name, but ›f calling me captain, he yelled out, "Hey, Birdie, did you news?" (The privates and non-coms called me Birdie a ıs long as my commanding officer wasn't around, it didn't ıe.) The kid told me about this big new kind of bomb that

Suited up and ready to go–only this time it's for Uncle Sam. Private Tebbetts is front and center.

I said "OK" and he said, "The fighting on Iwo Jima is going on right now, but it looks as though it will soon be coming to an end. And when the fighting is over, you go in and bring your team with you."

So I put my players on 24-hour alert and went back to guard duty. Long after dark a guy came up to me and said, "We're leaving in the morning. So get your men ready."

I said, "Yes, sir." Before dawn the next morning four or five trucks came up. We took all of our gear and threw it on the trucks and climbed on. Now my boys didn't know where they were going. I knew, but they didn't. And I was not supposed to tell anybody. It was dark and we drove out to the airstrip where there were four big four-engine B-24 bombers sitting there all ready to go. So we threw our stuff onboard–bases, balls, bats, and gloves–and the planes roared off into the dawn.

The planes leveled off at 8,000 feet, and as the day grew brighter the guys sprawled out on barracks bags and dozed off. I lay wondering what was in store for us and why this trip of ours to Iwo Jima was of concern to the top command.

The fighting on Iwo Jima had been some of the most ferocious of the war. It had been a Japanese stronghold, fortified with an underground complex dug deep into the soft volcanic rock. It was the base from which Japanese fighters had been attacking our B-29s on their way to Japan, and once the island was captured it would serve as a way station for our planes that couldn't make it back to the B-29 base on Tinian.

Our B-24s circled the pockmarked airstrip and put down for a bumpy landing. It was plain to see that just the day before our guys had been in the midst of a fierce battle; smoke was still rising from burnt-out emplacements and caves. The cost of the victory: more than 6,000 American kids dead.

As we climbed out of the planes and gathered up our gear we could stare up at Mount Surabachi, the site of that famous picture of the group of marines leaning together to raise the American flag. Surabachi is ugly. Black and volcanic. The Seabees (navy engineers) were our hosts. And I found out from them how we came to be there. When the marine commander was told that he could have a major league baseball game played right after the battle was over he said, "I need it. So many men are dead and dying, we need something to take their minds off what happened. Do whatever you need to do to get ready."

So with mortar shells still exploding nearby, the Seabees bulldozed a baseball diamond right out of that burned rock on Iwo Jima. I went out to look at it and I couldn't believe what I saw. The boundary of left field was the Pacific Ocean. The boundary of center field was the Pacific Ocean. The boundary of right field was the Pacific Ocean. They had chalk lines laid out along the base paths. We gave some Seabees our bases and a home plate and, presto, a playing field.

There was no way of announcing that there wa
game to be played. It had to be passed by word of m
game would be at such and such a time down b
Meanwhile, the Seabees got all of these empty bon
packing cases and put them around the diamond
them up about four feet from the baselines. They e
seats right behind the catcher.

When we got suited up and went out there to w
around and there were GIs and marines standing o
hanging off cranes, trucks, and jeeps. They were f
forms. Some covered with blood. They were walki
guns. The night before, they had a kamikaze att
turned out, was simple. To play ball. To put on a
game for 12,000 grimy, cheering, gun-toting, bat
and marines. To take their minds off the sheer ho
had just been through. They came on foot, by je
or two, and even some on crutches. It was an
They were lined up along the base paths, sitti
jury-rigged stands. Right behind home plate th
of shell cases as seating for VIPs.

When we were about to play the ballgame
over the loudspeaker, "On first base, Max W
Bees," and everybody yelled and cheered. "O
Gordon of the New York Yankees," and everyb
Howie Pollett and Tex Hughson," and they c
they announced the catcher, "Captain Bird
Detroit Tigers," and you never heard so many
You could hear it all over the South Pacific. It
boo an officer. A couple of guys from Provide
out of the ranks and said hello to me, and I l

Before starting the ballgame I looked arc
shots were sitting, right behind the catcher.
And when I said, "Oh, no, you can't sit the

a B-29 dropped on Hiroshima; the plane was flown by a Captain Tibbets. "That any relation of yours?"

"No." But I ran like hell to the barracks to tune in a radio to find out what this news meant.

It meant that the war would soon be over, and it meant that it would take time to bring home 15 million homesick GIs. It took about eight months after the war's end before I arrived at a discharge processing center in Greensboro, North Carolina. With baseball's Opening Day a few weeks away, it was a worry whether I'd make it in time. That mustering-out process takes maybe seven or eight days, standing in line, getting a physical, and getting this piece of paper stamped and that piece of paper stamped, and standing in line some more while a guy types this form and hands it to another guy who writes something on it and hands it to another guy. Finally I came to a guy who had to sign his name on a piece of paper so that it could be passed on to some other guy, and he looked up at me and said, "You are Captain Tebbetts?"

I said, "That's right."

He said, "I'm not going to sign this paper. I'm freezing your discharge. You're needed here in Greensboro. As a matter of fact, you aren't ever going to get out of the army, because I'm never going to sign this."

I said, "What the hell do you mean? I've got the points. I've served my time."

And he said, "I don't give a good goddamn, Tebbetts. I've got you by the ass. I'm keeping you in the army."

And I looked at him. There was something wrong here. I said, "What the hell is going on?"

And then he looked me straight in the eye and said, "Sid Hudson."

I said, "So you're that guy. The Pentagon guy."

He smiled and said, "So you can go and unpack your bags, Tebbetts, and settle in for a long stay."

I knew he couldn't keep me in the army forever, but he could stall my discharge for months so that I would miss baseball's Opening Day. I said, "We'll see about that." I went over to the PX, got five dollars worth of change, and went to the telephone booth to call Nashua, New Hampshire, and Paul Sadler, my old golfing buddy. He ran an insurance business and one of his agents used to sell policies to ballplayers on the side. Paul said to me, "Here's the number of New Hampshire Senator Stiles Bridges. Wait till Bridges hears about this!" So I called Washington, D.C., and a lady came on the line. I told her I was Birdie Tebbetts, and what the problem was, and that Opening Day was coming up fast. She said to hang up and not to move 10 feet from that pay phone until she called me back. So I sat down. I finally lay down and dozed off. And about six hours later the phone rang and it was Senator Bridges.

"Hello, Birdie, how are you? Here's what you do . . ."

The next morning I was sitting on my bunk at about seven in the morning when this guy came in and said, "Captain Tebbetts, grab your gear and follow me."

We went to the office of the Pentagon guy and he was sitting there all smug and knowing, and this guy walked up to him and handed him my papers and said, "Sign it."

And the Pentagon guy said, "I'm not going to sign it. Captain Tebbetts is needed here."

And the other man said, "Sign it. Orders of the commanding general."

The Pentagon guy looked at it and said, "I've never seen anything like this before."

And the guy said, "Sign it." And he signed it, and I walked out of the army and into the ballpark.

We went to war in a depression and came back to prosperity. Back home there was a lot of money and nothing to buy, so people went to the ballpark as never before. Back in civilian life and in the Detroit uniform, my old skills returned slowly. A new breed of Detroit fan booed me unmercifully. They were fans who had moved to the city and its defense industries and had become enamored of the wartime Detroit Tigers and resented their displacement by more skillful veterans.

Betty Tebbetts Deluca on

Life with Birdie

On Sunday mornings Dad would pile us in the car and drive us down to St. Barnabas. And we'd say, "Dad, aren't you coming in to church?" And he'd say, "I had a long talk with the Pope about my heart condition, and the Pope told me that instead of going to church I should take this little white pill, that taking this pill was the same as going to church. . See? I'm taking it now. So you go in there, say your prayers, and I'll be waiting outside when you come out."

And why not? The wartime Tigers had won a world championship, and Newhouser, Trucks, Trout, and so many other guys were around who had been exempt during the war and who, frankly, had on occasion told us they were sorry to see the war end as quickly as it did. They knew that as soon as it was over their ride was over. They did a lot of little things that burned us up, listening to how great they were when we knew that they were not for the most part major league–caliber baseball players.

One situation I ran into, and it was a situation that could have been unpleasant but was not because of the people who were involved, was the situation between Paul Richards and me. Now Paul Richards was a catcher. He had a major league arm. He could catch a ball and he could throw it, and that's about all he could do at the major league level. Ballplayers like Paul Richards before the war were a dime a dozen. He caught for the Atlanta minor league club down there in the Southern League. I believe he also managed that ballclub. He was one of the most brilliant minds in baseball. Richards always caught Newhouser. Newhouser had a winning career during the war, and Richards had been given all of the credit that he shouldn't have received, because Newhouser turned himself into a big winner. And it was a pretty well-known fact that, because of that combination, Richards was going to catch Hal Newhouser no matter what.

And that was OK with me. Soon after my arrival Paul came to me and we had a good long talk. He said, "Birdie, at my age I'm just riding out a couple of years here. I've had a great time, and I hope that they will allow me to catch Newhouser, and I hope you will catch everybody else." And I said that I would do nothing and say nothing that would indicate that I would like to catch Newhouser as long as that happened.

About midseason Paul came up with a deal to get some land down in Waxahachie, Texas, which he later converted into something very valuable for himself. But to do this deal he had to arrange his schedule so that (and we had talked this over) he would catch Newhouser on a Monday in Chicago, go to Waxahachie on Tuesday, Wednesday, and Thursday, then come back to catch Newhouser in St. Louis on Friday. And that was OK with everybody, except for one thing. It rained and we didn't play Monday. Richards had to stay over in Waxahachie and Newhouser had to pitch a game to me. He pitched a two-hitter, a brilliant game, and he won. The goings-on in Waxahachie were delayed and Paul missed the next Newhouser game where again Hal pitched brilliantly. Paul finally came back, but when it was Newhouser's turn to pitch again, Steve O'Neil, who was the manager, put my name in the lineup as catcher. I had told Steve that I didn't mind if he put in Paul, and Paul knew that I had said that. But Steve said, "No. We'll go along with you, Birdie, until Newhouser loses."

Now, I don't remember the sequence of wins and losses, but there came a time when Newhouser did not win, and Paul went in and caught him a couple of losers. But I caught him from then on, and when the season was over and they were talking about how Newhouser pitched brilliantly to Richards, the record of his pitching to me was something like 16 wins and 2 losses, and to Paul it was something like 5 wins and 7 losses. So the myth of Richards and Newhouser went out the window. And Richards would laugh about it every time we got together, because he went on to become a brilliant manager and general manager in the major leagues. He was just a great baseball guy, and we were good baseball friends.

Newhouser got into the Hall of Fame by begging to get into the Hall of Fame. And Newhouser was no more a Hall of Fame pitcher than was Schoolboy Rowe or Tommy Bridges. There was a guy named Ed Head who had pitched a no-hit, no-run game for Brooklyn and he was inducted into the army in Texas. I had a the army post team, and we faced Ed Head in a tournament down there after his no-hitter and beat him rather soundly. And then Howard Pollett, who was one of the really great pitchers, came into Texas to pitch in our semiprofessional atmosphere, and our army post beat him. Then they inducted Tex Hughson, who won 18 and lost 5 before he was inducted. An oil company paid him a lot of money to pitch a game against Waco Army Air Base and we beat every one of those guys. So I must say that if Hal Newhouser were pitching in Texas semipro or Texas service ball he might have had a little trouble winning. He was a good pitcher, but he was not the greatest left-handed pitcher in the world. And there are people I have caught whom I consider more qualified to be in the Hall of Fame than Hal Newhouser, because his record was almost completely a wartime record.

6

"Never interrupt your enemy when he is making a mistake."

–Napoleon Bonaparte

Catching Then and Now

Johnny Bench was right up there with Mickey Cochrane as probably the greatest catcher of all time–in all categories. I would say that Mickey was the better teacher of young talent. I would also say that the biggest difference between Mickey and Bench was the mitt. You look at the old pillow mitts that Mickey and I caught with and you can see that they require a whole different set of skills. Soft hands is what I call it. You had to bring a 100-mile-an-hour fastball into the pocket of the mitt without it popping out, and this meant having your throwing hand nearby and ready to grab the seams for a quick throw.

The new mitt, you look at it and it looks like an apple turnover or a soda biscuit. It's not much different from a first baseman's mitt, and as a result they've taken away so much and added so little to the art of catching. It's just that anybody can catch now. We are now taking a first baseman and putting him behind the plate. You never put a first baseman behind the plate before that banana mitt came in. The mitt was the thing.

You look at the pictures of the mitts we caught with and the way we held them waiting for a pitch, ready to draw the pitch in, and the way the right hand was there waiting to reach in and grab the ball by the seam, and you immediately see the difference in catching then and now. Roy Campanella showed me his mitt one time. It was filled with feathers.

Except for the design of the mitt, the catcher is the catcher he's always been. Remember that. Everything the catcher does is watched by eight members of the team. Any emotion that he goes through, disgust, anger, anything except confidence, is taking something away from somebody out there or adding to it.

If it's an important time in the ballgame and everybody is cheering like hell, and everybody is all uptight, and you're in Yankee Stadium in front of 60,000 people, before anything can happen the catcher has to sit down and give a sign. So everybody zeros in on the catcher. When the catcher goes down to give a sign, he can move the shortstop by just pointing a finger, which tells the shortstop to move over on the pitch. The last thing that the catcher does might make a difference.

The game can't start until everybody looks at the catcher. A catcher is the only guy that looks out and sees everybody else. The catcher looks out and sees Charlie Gehringer moving while he's giving a sign and he wonders what the hell Charlie's doing. Then suddenly there's a ball hit right to where Charlie moved to, and the catcher is the only son-of-a-bitch who saw him move! And then someone asks who was the best second baseman you ever saw, and you say Gehringer, and you can't recite the countless times over the course of a season you saw Gehringer move and have the ball drilled right to where he moved to. The catcher is the only one who noticed it.

Cochrane had a theory, and he was right. He said you should never throw a pitch 2 and 2 that you can't repeat 3 and 2. Suppose you have a count of 2 and 2 and you want to throw a

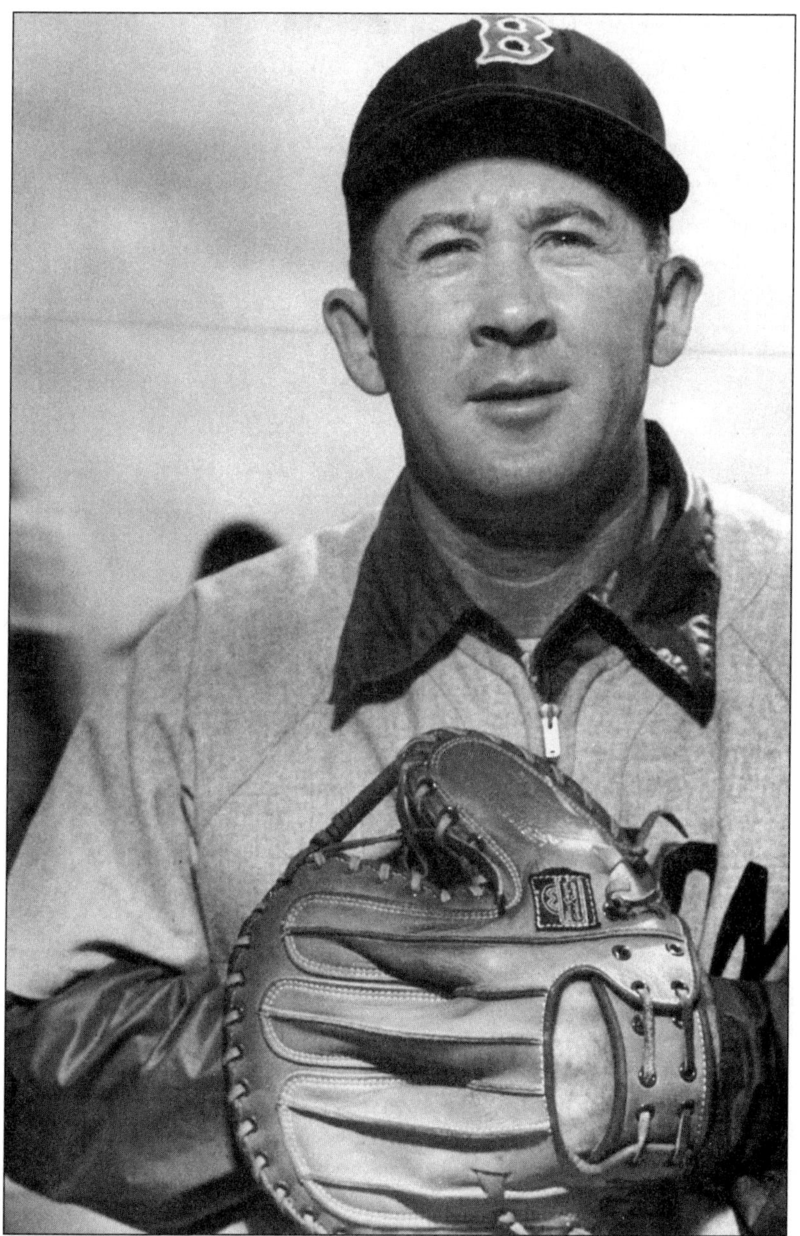

Me with one of the "pillow" mitts of yesteryear. Photo courtesy Frank Scherschel/TimePix.

curveball because you think the curveball will get the batter out, but you're not sure that your pitcher can throw a curveball strike. If you know that this batter is looking for a fastball and he's a good fastball hitter, you would like to call a curve 2 and 2 but then you have to throw the fastball 3 and 2. So you shouldn't have called for the curveball 2 and 2 because you won't be able to call the curve when it's 3 and 2. Don't ever do that. That point in a game is the most vital point in the count you can get into for the calling of a pitch.

Now that brings up the subject of left-hander Hal Newhouser. I mention Newhouser because in his first year up in a big game against Cleveland he insisted on trying to throw a third strike curveball and we lost. And I went up to the kid after the game and said, "You pitched well today, Hal. And a year from now we will win that ballgame." He took it wrong. He thought I was second-guessing, and it took a long time before we got it straightened out.

But I think the biggest difference now is what they're teaching these young catchers about framing the ball after it crosses the plate. It used to be you would catch a bad ball bad and a good ball good. You would catch a strike in the strike zone and you would catch a ball out of the strike zone. That meant if a ball was about that much outside, you caught it outside and you didn't sweep it in. That way, when you got into an inning where the bases were loaded, you had an umpire who had seen you catch without faking it, so when you catch this bad ball outside like this, he knows it's a ball. And then, when you get two strikes, you call the very same pitch and draw it in, and *instinctively* the umpire calls the pitch strike three–strike three when you really need it.

Now what they're teaching these young catchers to do–and it's so obvious that it's pathetic–they catch a ball that's outside and jerk it in. And the cameras are on it, and the fans see it, and everybody in the world sees that it's a ball, and they're trying to make a strike out of it! If you're catching and it's a ball and it doesn't mean that much, make a ball out of it! The umpire is going to like that. And when you really need it, you get a ball that far off, and he's expecting you to catch it in the ball zone, but instead you pull it in the strike zone, instead of saying, "Ball!" he says, "Strike!" He doesn't mean to say "strike" but he knows that up to that time you haven't been framing, so he thinks it's a strike. Catch the strike in the strike zone and catch the ball in the ball zone until you need a strike.

Susan Tebbetts Mitchell on

Life with Birdie

Picture Mom and Dad in our Florida home. And they are sitting on the porch in the evening, looking out to the canal. Mom says, "Birdie, where's the boat? Do you know where the boat is?"

He says, "Yeah. Some guys came to take it to fix it."

"What guys?"

"They came, they knocked on the front door and said, 'We're here to fix the boat.' I found the keys [he was proud of himself for finding the keys]. I got them the keys and they drove off."

"Jesus Christ! You gave the keys to the boat to thieves. The boat is gone! It's been stolen! Call the insurance company, but don't tell them you gave 'em the keys!"

You don't frame it. You don't catch a high fastball and move it in the strike frame. It's a good technique not to frame it and it creates a good image, and it will help you with the umpire as long as you catch all the time and you have the confidence of the umpire. You can do that with a real good umpire. And when the batter is heading back to the dugout, the umpire will lean down and whisper to you, "You bastard!" Or he may laugh and not say anything. He knows, but nobody is squawking. You try saying all that to a young catcher and he will wonder what the hell you're talking about.

I've made a big deal out of what makes the catcher and the catcher's view of the game different from that of any other player. But there is one other player, and only one, who shares that same viewpoint. That player is the umpire behind the plate. My point here is that the umpire deserves a separate chapter, and by God I'm going to give it to him.

7

"A baseball umpire is like a woman. He makes quick decisions, never reverses them, and doesn't think you're safe when you're out."

–Larry Goetz, veteran umpire

The Lawgivers

You have to admire the fact that a guy would begin his life wanting to be an umpire. There has to be something wrong with him to give up a normal way of life just for the love of the game. Umpires start out in the "kitty" leagues and move on to high school and college leagues. Then they go through the minor leagues just to be degraded, insulted, and taunted. Finally they get a chance in the big leagues only to find out that maybe they aren't capable of being in the big leagues. And if they do make the big leagues, they find they are living a very, very lonely life.

I don't expect the modern ballplayers to understand what it was like in my day because the attitudes are different now. And that is all because of the baseball umpire schools that came into existence to teach and inform and professionalize umpires, which they certainly did. They did a tremendous job of building up confidence and forming the major league umpires into a powerful organization. Good for them. But the first thing they learned when they went into the umpire training program, and they can disavow this if they wish, was to hate the ballplayer–hate him.

Umpires today have been taught to believe that the ballplayer is the son-of-a-bitch who is out to show up the umpire. That the ballplayer is always going to be against you. And that you can't get along with him and there's no use in trying, so as an umpire you must run him out of the ballpark before he runs you out of a job. But it wasn't always that way.

Chivalry at Home Plate

Somewhere I have a picture taken back in the thirties of a play at the plate, and in the picture is an umpire named Emmett Ormsby. Emmett was a Bill Harridge umpire who umpired mostly in Chicago. A White Sox umpire. Emmett had about 14 kids. He was an awfully nice man. Now I don't expect the umpires of today to understand what I'm talking about, nor do I think that the players of today could have the same kind of relationship we did in the thirties and forties before the war. So now you wonder what the hell this has to do with Emmett Ormsby and his kids?

I was a catcher. And a catcher is closer to an umpire, consistently, over a career than any other player. He's in constant touch. If an umpire wishes, and if a ballplayer is smart enough to understand the situation, there is a love-hate relationship that exists, and it all depends on the catcher. If the catcher will tell the umpire the truth, and tell him only the truth when he's talking to him head-to-head with nobody else listening, and keep it confidential, he will have a friend. He's not going to get any favors from the friend, but he will be able to understand. Everything in the ballgame goes along a helluva lot better if the catcher and the umpire tell the truth.

Now, about Emmett's big family.

The point is that it was in the middle of the worst depression the world has ever known, and anybody that had a job was lucky to have a job, and an umpire in the American League, if he was OK, would have take-home pay of $250 or maybe $300 a month. That's just during the season. So to keep 14 kids in feed, Emmett would buy everything by the case or by the dozen and even wholesale when he could do it. Emmett was also a veteran of World War I, and in 1918 in the trenches in the battle of the Somme he inhaled a whiff of phosgene gas, which seared the lining of his lungs. That often left him gasping and disoriented.

This one day in Chicago I was catching a ballgame in Comiskey Park, and Emmett was calling the game behind me. Early on, a guy hit a ball up the right-field line, and Emmett ran up the line to call it. When he came back he said to me, "Birdie, I'm getting very, very dizzy from the army thing, and I just don't know what to do about it. I can't see but I don't want to quit. I'm afraid if I do I'll lose my job."

And I said, "Are you all right? Are you going to be able to be steady on your feet, Emmett?"

He said he would be OK so I said, "Well, listen. When I raise my right hand it's a strike, and when I raise my glove it's a ball."

And before he could answer I got down and called for a pitch. When the pitch came in, I raised my right hand and he called it a strike. On the next one I raised my glove hand and it was a ball. And we went through the hitters of the inning that way.

Mike Tresh, who was catching for Chicago and who was a real dear friend of mine because we had been in the Detroit system together, came out and I said, "Mike, Emmett is sick and he can't see. If you raise your right hand it's a strike, and if you raise your glove it's a ball."

And he looked and nodded and said, "OK."

So I watched as the first hitter got up, and Mike went through the raising of the hand and the raising of the glove. It went on like that for a couple of more hitters, and then he

Susan Tebbetts Mitchell on

Life with Birdie

One Christmas Mom said, "You do the Christmas shopping, Birdie. You get the kids' presents."

So he said, "Oh, all right. Give me the sizes." So she gave him all the sizes–Susan is size 8, Betty wears size 5, and so forth. But when Christmas morning came, we opened up our presents and here were these little bitty sweaters, skirts, shirts. Kiddie clothes. He went to the kids department. We didn't have the heart to tell him. They were all returned, and he never knew.

stopped raising his hand and looked in to me and nodded to let me know Emmett was OK.

Emmett had made his recovery, and Mike and I got him out of a scrape. Years later I told that story to Dick Young of the *New York Daily News*. He printed it, and a lot of skeptics said such a thing couldn't happen. But let me tell you that under the system that existed in those days with Bill Harridge as the president of the league, and with Bill being the politician that he was, it not only could happen, it did happen.

Now as I'm telling that story I'm thinking about Roberto Alomar, who not too long ago, during a tantrum at home plate, had the bad manners to spit into the face of umpire John Hirschbeck. My first instinct was to ban the guy from baseball. It's disgusting. Doesn't matter that the playoffs were coming up. You can't tolerate that kind of behavior in professional sports. Similarly, it's not good to have a guy who's in charge of a major league baseball team come out and call an umpire a name that reflects badly upon him and his family. It should not be allowed and should be punished severely. Having said that, a ballplayer always has the right of appeal. It really gets political then; a contest between the umpires' union and the players' union. I don't know any more than that.

On the other hand, I don't think it's a good thing, what's going on now. Nowadays a hitter is not permitted to complain about a bad call. Nonsense. If a hitter can't complain about a called strike, who can complain when an umpire consistently calls a pitch wrong? If an umpire is consistently calling one pitch wrong, who's going to tell him he's doing it wrong? Cal Hubbard used to tell batters when they complained about a call, "Don't trust me. I'm liable to miss one. The strike zone is between those two white lines," meaning the inside of the batter's box. I'll give you an example from my era that used to happen quite often over the years.

The Elastic Strike Zone

On any given day when I was catching a ballgame, there's "Strike one!" And I might think to myself, "That's too low, Bill." "Strike two!" And I think, "That's too low, Bill." "Ball!" And my thought is, "That's too high, Bill." Meanwhile, just about every other batter is either yelling or giving the umpire dirty looks. About the third inning Bill might lean over and say, "Birdie, I'm getting a lot of complaints about the low strike." And without turning around I would say, "You're calling them wrong, Bill. Raise your strike zone."

Now everybody today is going to say that story is a fairy tale, but if you have been catching in front of a guy for, say, 10 years and you have passed the test of honesty, and you both understand that neither should pay a penalty because of your friendship, then it's not out of line. Cal Hubbard used to say, "If you can save getting in a fight with a catcher and pitcher, that's what's important. The hitter doesn't really know where it is." I can understand where a lot of people say it hasn't been done, but I'm saying it has been done.

Now, having said that, there are umpires who have very specific strike zones. They place themselves in a certain position and they watch for the ball to go through, and if the ball passes through that area where their strike zone is, it's a strike. And if it doesn't, it's a ball. And they miss some. But on the average, you can tell when a guy is a low-ball umpire or a high-strike umpire; there aren't very many high-strike umpires.

But all umpires want to be considered great umpires. That reputation is hard to come by, which introduces the George Robert Tebbetts pronouncement on what makes great umpires great. Are you ready?

Strike Four!

I always said that the great hitters–and when I talk about great hitters I mean the really great hitters, like Musial, DiMaggio, Williams, and this guy McGwire–they got four strikes at the plate, while the rest of us poor slobs got only three. And the reason I said that is because umpires hate to call strike three on great hitters. Here's what I mean.

This one day we were playing the Red Sox, and I was catching for Detroit and taking the warm-up pitches. Bill McGowan, who was a very good friend of mine, was behind me calling balls and strikes. I said to Bill, "Ted Williams is coming up, and I bet you wouldn't have the guts to call him out on strikes." He just said, "Play ball, Mr. Tebbetts." Now Ted ran the count to 3 and 2, and the next pitch came in that far off the plate, and Bill yelled, "Strike three!"

Ted just looked at him and walked off, and then Bill said to me, "That's the last time that is going to happen, Mr. Tebbetts. Thirty thousand people are out there. They didn't come here to see you catch, and they sure as hell didn't pay to see me call balls and strikes. They came out to see Ted Williams hit. And from now on, that's what they're going to get."

An umpire feels that when dealing with a great hitter, he is a great umpire. I think that is the relationship an umpire unconsciously has when he's dealing with the great ballplayers. How often does it happen? It happens with a DiMaggio, it happens with the Mantles, and it happens with the Williamses. They don't want to be a lousy umpire who would call out a great hitter. They want to be a good umpire who would give them a chance to hit. It's a simple way of saying it, but it's a simple statement of fact. Great hitters make great umpires out of ordinary ball-and-strike callers. They let 'em hit.

The Stickler

It's terribly important when you're playing baseball to understand the umpire and what he stands for and what makes each guy tick. They are all different. There was a guy named Farley out of Worcester, Massachusetts, and he was so quick on the trigger I could never figure him out. I used to run across him during the winter on the banquet circuit and he was such a nice guy. But once that ballgame started, he was a terrier. He would get as heated up over a tiny little infraction as he would with a major one. He was always looking for trouble. That's the only way I could figure him out. And then I found out that if you lived exactly by the rules, you had no trouble with him.

To test this out, one day when I was managing I had one of my players toss a uniform jacket on the top step of the dugout. That particular day this guy Farley was umpiring third base. Well, he looked over at the dugout, saw this jacket on the top step, called time, and made a beeline for me. When Farley got about 10 steps away, my ballplayer snatched the jacket off the step. At that Farley stopped dead in his tracks, looked over and saw me grinning, and then nodded, turned, and went back to work. From that experiment I learned something important about the umpires who were sticklers.

When Tempers Flare

Roy Weatherly played for Cleveland, and he should have been one of the really great players. But Weatherly had a peculiar disposition. His temper was set on a hair trigger. For some reason

Cal Hubbard, the umpire, had worked a long series of games with the Cleveland ballclub, and in those games he had called Weatherly out on a couple of pitches that Roy thought were not strikeout pitches, and Roy became pretty upset. Hubbard was about 6'4" or 5" and Roy was about 5'7". But Roy gave Cal hell, and Cal gave him hell back. It got to the point where this one day Weatherly was warned by the league that if he complained anymore about any pitch, he was out of the ballgame.

Well, we found out about that, and Weatherly was first up in this particular game I was catching in Cleveland. The very first pitch of the ballgame was called a strike. There was no question it was a strike. Big and juicy and right down the middle. I took one step up until I was level with Roy, and before I threw the ball back I glanced at him, opened my eyes wide, and turned around with a little shake of my head. Weatherly stepped out of the box and took a couple of little dance steps and then got back in the box.

Lo and behold, a few moments later here comes another pitch, and Hubbard calls, "Strike." And I do the same thing, sort of shaking my head at Weatherly, and he falls for it, hook, line, and sinker. This time he is about to say something to Cal, but the guy in the on-deck circle runs up and gets him to quiet down. Now we come to the third strike, and I don't remember whether it was down the middle or not. But when I caught the ball, I stepped forward and said, "Uh oh!" and Weatherly threw his bat up in the sky and said, "I knew it!" He looked right at Cal and said, "You big fat son-of-a-bitch!"

Hubbard just stood there and looked at him and said, "You're done, Weatherly. Get the hell outta here."

Well, just before it got out of hand, the Cleveland coaches escorted Roy away from Cal. The game was about to go on when Hubbard leaned over to me and said, "Birdie, I saw what you did, you nasty little shit." And we both had a laugh. But it was done, and it was funny, and I didn't try it again.

Swinging in the Rain

According to the rules, the home team owns the baseball game until it gives the ball to the umpire, at which time the umpires are in control of the game. Before that the team can call off the game if it wants or, depending on the circumstances, let the game go on. I will always remember one time in Detroit when it was raining awfully hard, but the stands were full with a good paid attendance. The Detroit ballclub did not want to call the game, but they didn't want the responsibility for starting the game in such a heavy rain either. So the manager, Mickey Cochrane, gave the ball to Cal Hubbard and said, "Cal, they want to play the game."

Hubbard said, "Mickey, you can tell them they're going to play the goddamn game, no matter what!"

And Mickey said, "OK, we understand."

Now the game started, and the going was so slippery around home plate that we slipped and slid on almost every step. We had to hit flat-footed. The pitching mound was so heavy with mud that the pitcher couldn't plant his foot. He just slid and threw the ball, and not too hard or he'd fall on his ass. So that particular day there were more home runs hit than I ever remember. But we played and we played and we played. Roxie Lawson was the pitcher for Detroit, and I finally said to Cal, "How long, Cal?" and he said he'd let me know.

So we're playing and we get into the situation where we've gotten a certain number of outs. The game is a legal game, but Hubbard makes us play on. It was so bad that when Jerry Walker ran in from left field he saw a big puddle, dove in head first, and made like he was swimming. That got a lot of laughs from the stands and it made the papers. Anyway, the game was legally complete, and it was getting ridiculous, and finally Hubbard told me, "You tell Roxie to throw three straight balls into the screen and to take a little time wiping his hands between pitches, and then I'll call it."

Roxie threw the ball into the screen, shook his head, wiped the ball, threw another and another into the screen, and Hubbard turned around, threw up his hands, and majestically called the game, and the Detroit Tigers were able to bank their paid attendance.

That was the worst baseball game I was ever forced to play, and it came about by virtue of the home club's possession of the ball. But Cal was going to give the public the game it paid to see.

Sometimes Blind

During a series at Fenway in Boston one season I was catching with Charlie Berry umpiring behind me and Lou Boudreau hit a home run that went past the foul pole. It was foul and everyone saw it was foul–everyone except Charlie Berry. He called it fair. And before the series was over, he told me his sight line got blocked on the play. There was nothing I could do or say about it. He knew I wouldn't say anything. He just wanted it to be a matter of record between him and me. "Birdie, that home run, you blocked me out on the play. Stay down!" And that was OK. I said nothing about it. But years later, after I became a manager, the lesson was very useful.

Whenever I went out as a manager to talk to an umpire, I wanted to know 1) if he was in position to call the play, and 2) if he was in position, did he really see the play or was he blocked out. And if the answer was that he was in position to see the play and was not blocked out, then there was nothing I could do about it. He saw it and called it the way he saw it. Whether he was right or wrong, he did his job the best he could. That is the way I treated a decision at first base and home plate. In any case, it's always important to try your best not to embarrass an umpire or, as we say in baseball, to "show him up."

I'll give you an example of how easy it is for an umpire to get the wrong idea. Lee Ballanfant was calling a game when I first managed at Cincinnati, and Lew Burdette was pitching against us for Milwaukee. Now Lew Burdette had a reputation for loading up a ball just before he threw, and although I wasn't so sure about that, I thought that his reputation might give me some kind of advantage if I used it right. Ballanfant and I had known each other since my Texas League days. Anyway, about the fifth inning the game was not going our way. I called time just before Burdette started his windup, and I went out and told Ballanfant that there was something on the ball. So he asked Burdette for the ball and looked at it and showed it to me, and there was nothing on it so I walked back to the dugout.

A while later, I came out a second time and told Lee there was something on the ball. And he said, "I'm goddamned if I'm going to look at that ball again." But I'd noticed that Burdette was getting irritated when I came out the second time, so after a while I came out a third time, hoping to upset his concentration. Well, this time Ballanfant just blew.

"Look, Tebbetts. I'm in charge of this ballgame, and I think you're trying to show me up. One more time and you're going to the showers. Now get the hell off the field." I didn't say another word, realizing my ploy backfired and jeopardized my standing with Ballanfant. Umpires do not like to be showed up. Ever.

A Scout in Blue

You ever hear of umpires acting as scouts? It was not unheard of in the old days. I was doing badly in Detroit right after coming out of the service. My catching skills had lost their edge, my hitting was off, and the fans were riding me. Then gradually I began to get sharper, and eventually I regained my old form. Bill Summers was umpiring in Detroit one day, and he asked me how everything was. I told him that I was very unhappy playing for Detroit but that the skills I had before the war had nearly returned, and I was beginning to play well again.

He said, "Well, if you feel that way, how much longer are you going to play?" I told him that I thought I could play four or five more years because I was in good shape.

Now, at the time it seemed to me to be nothing more than a conversation we had while standing around home plate. But on the next trip, we played three games in Boston, and after the last game, as usual, we showered and went down to South Station to take the train to New York.

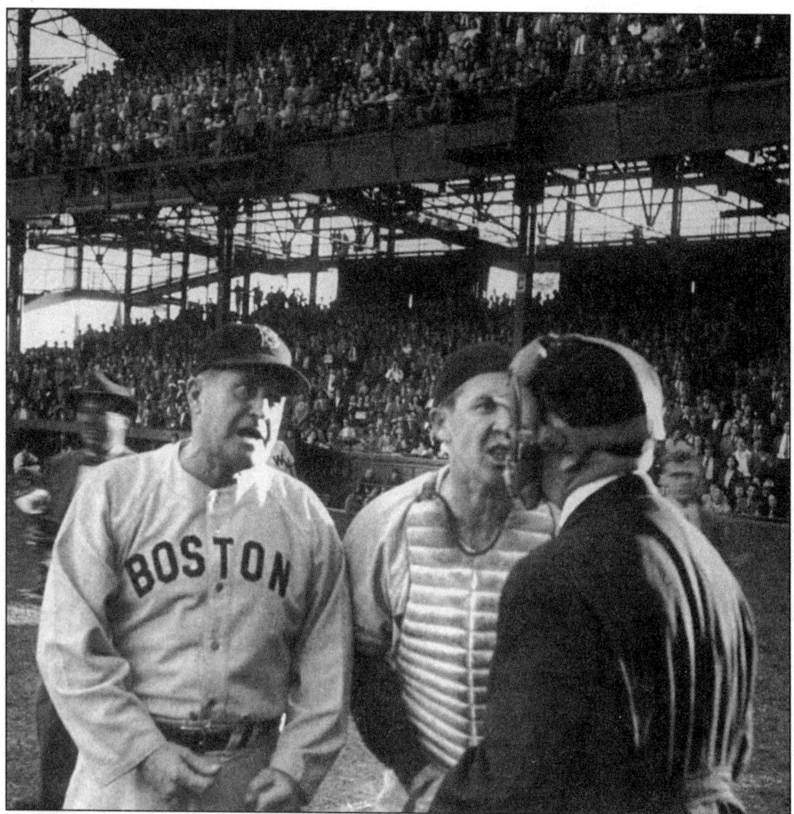

Me and Red Sox manager Joe McCarthy "advise" ump Bill Grieve about the dimensions of the strike zone. Notice the photographer moving about freely on the field behind McCarthy; this was a practice the league banned after I became a manager. Photo courtesy Michael Rougier/TimePix.

The routine was that the traveling secretary would always see to it that our luggage was picked up in the morning at our hotel and loaded into the baggage car of the train. But when I got to South Station and walked down the ramp to get onboard, I saw my bag sitting all alone out on the platform. For some reason somebody must have pulled it out of the baggage car and left it there.

That's how I found out I got traded. But I didn't know yet where I had been traded to. Cleveland was coming in, and I thought that was a possibility. But when I got to my luggage, the traveling secretary told me I had been traded to the Red Sox. So I was already where I was traded to. The point of the story is that the next time Bill Summers umpired a game for the Red Sox, he said to me, "I turned out to be a pretty good scout, didn't I, Birdie?"

I said, "What do you mean, Bill?"

And he said, "Well, before I went in to umpire your series in Detroit, Joe Cronin and I were talking and he said, 'I'd like to know if you could find out what kind of shape Birdie is in and how he feels about continuing to play, because we have an interest in him and I don't want to interfere with him or his plans. But anything you want to say on this is OK.' I told Cronin exactly what you had said to me and two days later you were traded. So I considered myself an outstanding scout on the basis of what you've been doing for the Red Sox." That was a time when umpires would scout for major league ballclubs.

Horsing Around

On one particular day, my mother was in Boston watching a game. Bill Summers and I were very friendly during the off-season, and I got to know his wife because she would accompany him to some of the banquets where he and I spoke. One day in Fenway Park while Bill and I were standing around home plate and I was taking some warm-up pitches, Bill mentioned to me that his wife was at the game and wanted him to say hello to me, and I said, "OK, Bill, thank you very much." Then I turned around and saw my mother and Bill's wife sitting very close to each other in the stands, and I told Bill, "My mother and your wife are pretty close over there, Bill."

When we got into about the fifth or sixth inning, Bill said to me, "Our women folk are sitting together. Looks like they're having a nice talk, Birdie." And I glanced around and saw my mother visiting with Mrs. Summers, and I started to grin. I said, "Bill, let's get into a fight. You face the stands where the women are, because you're going to do all the hand waving and everything else, and watch what their reaction is."

So there was a pitch called and I raised hell about the pitch, and he tore off his mask and started waving it around, all the while looking at the two women in the stands. And he's saying to me, "Boy we broke up that conversation, Birdie. You ought to take a look at this. They're not talking anymore. They're looking away. They don't know what to do. Let's call a truce before they become enemies." We both started to laugh and got on with the game. I think that camaraderie is a part of umpiring that we will probably never see again.

Another day I slid into second base and looked up at umpire Ernie Stewart thumbing me out, but he yelled "Safe!" I said, "What the hell is going on, Ernie?" He said, "You're safe, but 30,000 people saw me call you out, so you're out."

The thing that I love about the umpire is the trust that we put in him, and the things that he must go through. If the tables were reversed, I don't know whether we could have ourselves under that kind of control. Suppose you're an umpire and a guy is walking up to you and he's mad as hell. There is no love lost between you, so this guy calls you a blind bastard, and that's OK. But when he gets right up in your face and says, "You're a blind son-of-a-bitch!" it's amazing to me that umpires haven't hauled off and belted somebody. Sometimes I wonder why they think it's worth it to take that stuff. Especially if they don't get the backing from their front office.

I guess the point is that you have to really love the game to be an umpire. At one time some experts were really advocating playing the game without umpires. Now that's lunacy.

When Wives Matter Most

I was walking through the lobby of our hotel in Chicago one afternoon and ran into Bill Harridge, president of the American League. At the time I was second-string catcher to Jim Hegan for Cleveland, and my baseball career would soon be coming to an end. Mr. Harridge invited me to sit down for a chat over a cup of coffee, and he asked me what my plans might be after I retired from the game. I mentioned that the possibility of managing was in the offing, and he said, "Well, that all sounds fine and I hope it works out for you. But I want you to know that if you might want to become an umpire in the American League, there's a job for you after you've had a few months working in the minors." Well now, by then I had a bunch of kids and a wife who worries, and here's a man who has to be taken seriously. So I told Mary, my wife, about the offer, and we put the idea on the shelf for a while.

Then one evening Mary and I were having dinner in a restaurant in Cleveland. We had just been seated when I noticed that umpire Jim Honochick was dining alone nearby, so I invited him to join us. We got to talking about heated arguments we'd been in, and this went on, and at one point Mary said to Jim, "What's the worst situation you've ever been in?"

Jim didn't hesitate. I remembered reading the story, but I never thought to ask Jim about it. It was when he had just started umpiring in the big leagues and was working a game in Washington, the nst Cleveland. In the eighth inning with the score 0–0, obinson, the Washington first baseman, was on third. A guy hit a grounder and they caught Robinson in a rundown between third and home when he ran smack into Cleveland's pitcher, Early Wynn, who was standing in the middle of the base path *without the ball.*

Honochick waved his arms and said to Robinson, "You score!" As soon as he said that, the entire Indians bench came out whooping and hollering. So there were all these guys yelling and shoving at Jim like they were about to kill him while he tried to explain to Lou Boudreau, the Cleveland manager, how he'd called the play. Finally, after Boudreau cleared his guys back, Jim explained the difference between *obstruction* and *interference.* Since Wynn didn't have the ball, blocking the base path was considered obstructing the runner, and according to the rule book this did not kill the ball, it allowed the runner to advance. Interference automatically kills the ball. Well, nobody had ever heard of this rule before, and nobody had ever seen it applied until this rookie umpire came along and enforced it.

I thought Jim's story was interesting but not very frightening and was tempted to repeat the one Mary had heard a thousand times about the guy in Cleveland who dropped a pail of garbage on my head. Instead I decided to top Jim with a different story, the tale of a sweltering Sunday afternoon in Yankee Stadium.

To really appreciate this story you have to remember what was going on in the world then. It was the summer that France fell to the Nazis, and it's hard to believe nowadays, but that caused a street celebration in the German section of Manhattan and ended up in a bigger celebration in Times Square. It was a time of mean spirits. America was split between those who were against getting involved in the war and those who thought we ought to do something. And there were not many for doing something.

So on that Sunday in 1940 it was hotter than hell and 68,000 angry fans were crammed into Yankee Stadium. Detroit was leading the league at midseason and the Yanks were in fourth place. And, as I say, the fans were not happy after their team lost the first game of this doubleheader. Making matters worse, the Yankees were behind by one run in the second game. Now with two on base, Yankee Tommy Henrich hit a shot down the right-field line that tipped Rudy York's glove, and both runners scored. But umpire Joe Rue called the drive a foul from home plate and sent back the runners, setting off an explosion from Yankee coach Earle Combs at first base. Joe McCarthy joined in. Everybody was yelling and then the fans joined in, throwing half-eaten sandwiches, beer bottles, scorecards, programs, and seat cushions–and then the fruit started flying. It got so bad that Detroit manager Del Baker called his players off the field and the Yankees retreated to their dugout along with umpires. All except Joe Rue, who had called the play.

That little guy, built like a fireplug, stood right there at home plate with his arms folded, looking straight ahead and defying the whole screaming mob. Meanwhile people in box seats started getting hit with debris and had to retreat to the rear grandstands. This went on for maybe 15 minutes, whooping and booing and hollering, until finally the New York police sent a uniformed emergency squad into the ballpark and things quieted down. It took the groundskeepers another 20 minutes to clean up the field before play could start again. Detroit won both games. The next day John Kiernan, a good friend of mine and a sportswriter for the *New York Times*, printed a piece saying that Rue's firm stand at home plate was the bravest thing he'd ever seen on a ball field. What the story could not report was that Rue's salary for assuming the responsibility for the integrity of the entire baseball industry was less than $100 a week.

When I finished telling that story, Honochick agreed that he had never had to handle a crowd the way Joe Rue did. Then we finished our coffee and went our separate ways.

That night before turning in, Mary said she'd never heard that story about Joe Rue and the riot in Yankee Stadium. I didn't say anything, but then she added, "I don't care if you have to go back to selling insurance, you're not going to be an umpire."

8

"It is foolish and childish, on the face of it, to affiliate ourselves with anything so insignificant and patently contrived and commercially exploitative as a professional sports team . . . and the icy scorn of the nonfan is . . . almost unanswerable. Almost. What is left out of this calculation, it seems to me, is the business of caring; caring deeply and passionately, really caring–which is a capacity or an emotion that has almost gone out of our lives."

–Roger Angell

At Home in the Fens

I was batting .094 when Detroit traded me to the Red Sox in May of 1947. By the end of the season I had hit .299 for them. I was playing with a great ballclub for an old friend, Joe Cronin, and a rich and generous owner, Tom Yawkey.

My Red Sox years were the golden ones. The team was always in contention. I was close to home, among friends, popular in New England, and playing at the top of my form. And to top things off, in 1948 Joe McCarthy became our manager, and I learned from him most of what it takes to manage a ballclub.

That year the Red Sox acquired a right-hander from the St. Louis Browns, and he was a hell of a pitcher. He was also tall and handsome and a snappy dresser. He also took himself very seriously. One day in the clubhouse when everybody was milling around waiting for our turn at taking practice, the new guy, Jack Kramer, was bragging about this shopping spree he had been on the day before. He said he bought two suits, half a dozen trousers, and four sport coats, and he went on like this. The clothes were being altered and he couldn't wait to show them off. He said, "Best looking clothes you'll ever see, but you bunch of hillbillies wouldn't know the difference, so what the hell." Well, a week later Jack announced he would be picking up his new clothes. So the next day I was in the clubhouse before Kramer arrived, and I said to Ted Williams, "Kramer is coming in pretty soon and he'll be wearing his new clothes. Now no matter what I say to him I want you to agree with me." And Ted said "OK."

Pretty soon Kramer came waltzing in and sure enough he was all decked out in a flashy sport coat and greenish trousers with a knife crease in them. He stood in the middle of the room and all eyes were on him, and he turned in a circle with his chest out and said, "All right, you assholes, what do you think?" I went up to him and felt the material and said, "Gee, they are beautiful, Jack. Must have cost you a fortune. What do you think, Ted?" Ted said, "Yeah, they're beautiful, Birdie. Must have set him back a pile." Then I stood back and frowned and said, "Wait a minute, Jack. The left sleeve is longer than the right." And Ted said, "Gee, you're right, Birdie." Then I reached up and adjusted Jack's collar and said, "Jack, your collar is riding up." Ted came up and looked at it and said, "That's right, Birdie, but have you looked at the trousers? The cuff is riding too high." Jack looked down at his trouser cuffs, and he walked to the mirror and turned this way and that. The rest of the guys were having a hell of a laugh without letting on, and Jack slinked off cussing out his tailor. I really felt sorry for that poor tailor when Jack Kramer got through with him, but we all had a good laugh. Jack won 18 games for us that year.

Tebbetts Night at Fenway

"Tebbetts Night." They proclaimed it with a lot of hoopla. I was to be "honored" at home plate and given gifts galore. These events are stunts to give the local merchants, politicians, and

With Boston teammate and first baseman Walt Dropo, passing the time on the overnight train to Chicago. The years spent with Boston were golden. Photo courtesy Francis Miller/TimePix.

fraternal organizations a chance to share the spotlight with a hometown boy who has made good. You know you are being used, but that's OK as long as everybody has a good time and nobody gets stung. The working stiffs of Nashua, New Hampshire, chipped in to buy their guy a new Buick Roadmaster convertible. All this was to be presented ceremoniously at home plate prior to the National Anthem. And there I was, standing like an altar boy, cap in hand in the Red Sox uniform, grinning with head slightly bowed and deferential as New Hampshire's governor got in the act with "a few words," as did Nashua's mayor and a few other big shots. Then I went to the mike, smiling broadly while the flashbulbs popped, and thanked the governor, the mayor, and all of my friends from Nashua and said something nice about God. When I finished, everybody stood and cheered, and finally the groundskeepers pushed the car off home plate and the game began. To top off the evening, in the sixth inning I hit a double to right off Dick Fowler. Ma told me after the game that the ancient Connie Mack came up to her in the stands and said how do you do.

The Ban

I don't think many people think much about the close connection between the press and the spectator-sport industries. When I say "the press" I'm talking about television and radio but especially newspapers. The media and the sport industries are interdependent. Every guy buys a paper in the morning and the first thing he turns to is the sports page to look at the box scores. And on the way to work he reads what this writer or that writer has to say so that when he gets to work he can argue with another guy at the water cooler about yesterday's game and whether the manager pulled the pitcher too soon or too late. Everybody has an opinion. A guy may buy only two tickets a year, but that's OK. He buys *papers* every day, so the newspapers are happy, the advertisers in the papers are happy, and the two tickets make ballclubs happy. Because while the guy is at the ballpark he buys a scorecard, a couple of hot dogs, and two tonics (that's the same as soda pop for folks who don't live in Boston). And if the ballplayer is very lucky and thoughtful on how he handles the sportswriters, the ballplayer can be happy too. Good press is a player's currency. He can cash it in. Because if the ballplayer gets good things written about him, he is popular and fans come to see him play. When that happens he can demand and get more money out of an owner who is a tightwad and eccentric. It is a closed-end economic system. What's good for the game is good for the papers is good for the game is good for the papers is good . . . It goes round and round. But 50 years ago when Ted Williams was the star of the Red Sox, television counted for little and there were too many papers and too many sportswriters chasing too few stories. The really big story in those days was anything Ted Williams did. And if he didn't do anything, they would write stories about what he ought to do or what he might do or what they thought he was thinking of doing.

Susan Tebbetts Mitchell on

Life with Birdie

He used to buy stuff. He'd go to the funky stores and the sidewalk sellers. He saw these straw purses, stuff that we would never carry, and he would say, "I'll give you a buck for each of them. Give me three." And he'd collect these bizarre things and would come home with a big smile. "What did you get us, Dad?" And we'd unwrap these funky purses and say, "Thank you, thank you, Dad." We never told him. We never hurt his feelings. But he was always proud of his bargains. He'd say, "You know, I got that three for a buck." Nobody else's dad behaved the way he behaved. He was a funny guy. When Mom made him cook dinner he'd have the fried chicken contest. "It's my turn to cook dinner. It's another contest. We're going to have the fried chicken contest!"

Who are ballplayers? It seems like a dumb question, but think about it for a while and you come to realize that ballplayers are entertainers. Then you ask yourself the next question which is, How does the public get to know about the entertainer if he's just an ordinary ballplayer who doesn't hit a home run every day? The answer is the newspapers and the sportswriters. What I'm saying is that good publicity is important to a ballplayer's career. I learned early on how important it was to play as best I could and at the same time get as good press coverage as I could in every city where I played. To do that I had to learn how to appreciate the sportswriter's problem, which is to come up with interesting stories every day of the week. That's how the guy makes his living, and if

John Kiernan, legendary columnist for The New York Times, *saying something to make two rivals smile.*

I could help a guy and he could help me without doing any damage to another player then everybody is happy as hell.

Now about some of my favorite writers. John Kiernan of *The New York Times.* He was not only a great sportswriter, he was also a special kind of genius because he was on a very popular radio show in the thirties and forties called *Information Please,* a panel show where these brainy wizards would recall and recite from memory obscure passages from Shakespeare, the Bible, poetry, or even baseball statistics. Some of the other great writers in New York at the time were Arthur Daley of *The New York Times* and of course Red Smith, who wrote brilliantly for *The Herald Tribune.* Jimmy Cannon was another great writer. I think those men were kind to me because I was able to give them not only stories but also insights that they could develop into full columns. I doubt whether I could have attained whatever success I had as a player or a manager without fair treatment of the press. And I got it. Most of the time.

Which brings up the subject of my friend and teammate Ted Williams, who didn't get fair press any of the time. At least not in Boston, which had more newspapers and sportswriters than it needed. Boston was hungry for stories about the Red Sox. Hell, all of New England was hungry for news of the Sox. And it didn't matter whether the stories were true, false, speculation, rumor, or innuendo. The competition among writers of stories about the Red Sox was so ferocious that somebody had to put on the boxing gloves and somebody had to dish out the honey. There were people in Nashua, New Hampshire, who would gather at 1:00 in the morning at the station where they dropped off bundles of the next morning's Boston papers. All this fuss just to be the first to read "Colonel" Dave Egan's column in the *Record* about the Red Sox. Egan was a writer of brilliant vitriol. Harvard Law, a drunk, a cruel rogue who hated Ted Williams, Egan once called Ted "the inventor of the automatic choke." And too many Red Sox fans were ready to enjoy if not believe what he wrote.

And it wasn't just Egan. Roger Birtwell was one of the writers there who didn't know what the hell he was talking about, and he would walk around the clubhouse not asking any questions but listening to ballplayers talk to one another. Then in the next day's paper he would quote them as saying such and such a thing, printing something when what was printed was said confidentially one person to another. We called him a keyhole writer. He wasn't a bad guy. He didn't write what he thought. He wrote what he heard in innocent conversation.

Naturally I'm not saying every writer was hard on Williams. I'm talking about those writers who went out of their way to focus on Williams' private life. It was foul. It was cruel. They interfered with his personal life. They interfered with his marriage. They interfered with his family situation. And they never ever gave the guy credit for his personal commitment during the war. He was a marine fighter pilot, a hero in World War II at the peak of his baseball career. And then he was called back to fight the Korean War. He served with John Glenn over Korea. And he served his country without complaint. I think he lost six years during the height of his career to the military. That's Ted Williams for you. Yet there never was an editorial comment about what Ted did when his country needed him.

You only need a few writers in a city to take out after a ballplayer to seriously affect the way he is treated by the fans. So Ted wanted to get even. He wanted to ban every goddamn sportswriter from the clubhouse. He wanted writers kept out after a ballgame because that's when and from where all of the nasty stories seemed to originate. He had talked to all of the players individually and told them what he wanted, asking them to vote with him. He got just enough guys to say they would vote with him, and then he told Dominic DiMaggio, who was our representative, that he wanted to have a meeting.

Before the meeting Ted came to me and said, "This is what I'm going to do, Birdie, and I have enough votes to get the job done." I told him he was making a mistake. And he said, "I'm not making a mistake, Tebbetts. You're the newspaper boys' pet, and you love them. And if you are against the ban, God damn it, you are as bad as they are." Now this was my friend giving me hell. It hurt.

I told him that although I thought he was wrong, if he felt as strongly as he did, I would not vote against him, but that he was going to hurt some of the newer and younger players on the club. He asked, "Well, you're not going to speak against it, are you?" And I said, "No. Not unless you want me to. So don't call on me or I will."

At the meeting there were 25 guys sitting around in front of their lockers. All of the clubhouse people were told to go out and get a smoke. Before the vote was taken Williams got up and gave a speech about what lying bastards the writers were and that we don't have to take it from them, and the way to solve the problem was to ban them from the clubhouse. And as he was giving his talk I sensed that the ban was going to be passed as a favor to Ted. He must have sensed that he was going to carry the vote, and he turned to me and said, "I know you don't agree with me, Tebbetts. You're a newspaper lover. You're their baby Birdie. How do you feel about this?"

I looked up and said, "Ted, you and I had an agreement and now it no longer exists." And then I said, "I want all of you to listen very closely. None of us are great ballplayers when we are compared to Ted Williams. Ted Williams is as great a ballplayer as ever lived. And he certainly is as great a player as there is in the game and probably is the best. And he cannot do anything that they can totally criticize. And if he does, it's not going to bother him in one way or another. The fans will get upset when this man or that man accuses Ted of not trying or whatever." I singled out players, including myself, saying, "I need newspapermen to write about what I do. I'm happy with what they write when I do well and I feel badly when they write when I don't do well. I think it's terribly important for players like me to be well thought of by the press without selling out our souls. I think if all you guys who are in this room would look at yourselves you'd find out that you are all about like me, but there is only one Williams. Ted called on me and I'm telling you that if you ban the newspapermen you will be terribly hurt in your entire career. And if you have a good day and they don't give you the credit you deserve–and you won't get it if you ban them–then when it comes time to talk contract, management will remind you that you were not liked and the fans booed you. It once happened to me. They booed Greenberg and me out of Detroit. And it may last your lifetime, because when you go back to your hometown the newspapermen there will not understand that we voted for the ban as a favor to Ted. I'm telling you that I'm going to vote to keep them in." It got quiet, and every guy wrote something on a piece of paper and Dominic counted. And Ted lost.

Needless to say, Ted went into a rage and called me every kind of a son-of-a-bitch he could think of, and I somehow let it pass.

About a month later he came to me. "I'm going to have our next meeting," he said. "I'm going to bring up the banning again. Now, you told me last time you wouldn't talk." And I said, "Hey, Ted, you asked me to talk." Well, he said, "I'm not going to ask you this time and I'd appreciate it if you didn't." So I said I wouldn't "but you better have the vote taken by a show of hands. Ask those who are going to vote for a ban to raise their hands." The vote was taken by a show of hands, and everybody could see whose hand went up and whose hand did not. And the ban was passed.

Now, in that second meeting there were three hands not raised. Mine and Lou Stringer's were two of them. Lou had just come over from the Cubs, and he said he was not in a position to antagonize anyone, and he therefore voted to allow them in. I have never told anyone who cast the third vote, so if somebody reads this asking who was the third man, anybody could claim to be the one. The ban went into effect, and the newspapers raised hell.

Then all of a sudden up in the front office Cronin, McCarthy, and Yawkey, who all tried to stay out of it, suddenly realized what a bad thing it was for the gate, the attendance. When the newspapermen drew back and weren't allowed in, you can imagine the kinds of stories that did not get printed because their sources dried up. Then the word came down from above: it's your business, but Tom Yawkey would like to have a settlement that allows there to be a time limit after a game when players can unwind and settle down and not be bothered by the guys who were looking for the sensational remark that guys are apt to make in the five or ten minutes after the game. And the time was set and fundamentally agreed upon as half an hour or an hour after the game that they couldn't come in. That satisfied the front office to a certain degree.

The funniest part of the story is that after the news got out that they had been banned, we walked through the runway to get to the dugout and a couple of newspapermen were waiting at the end of the bench. They were the scorekeepers. They were not the regular press, but they were there to represent those who were. And the question they asked each guy was, "How did you vote?" You would be surprised how many guys said they voted to keep them in when there were only three of us who actually did vote to keep them in. They didn't want to take the rap.

I don't blame Ted, but I do blame the ballplayers who voted with Ted. Because I don't think anyone other than Ted had any kind of complaint about a personal attack from a writer of the kind done to Ted. In any case, baseball learned something from the episode. But not the press and here's why.

Those of us who played with Ted will never forget the fact that Ted lost the Most Valuable Player award because just one single Boston writer, out of personal dislike, refused to vote for him even as the *10th* most valuable player. Ted missed out by that one vote. The prize would have been his if this one guy had voted for Ted as the 10th most valuable player and he wouldn't do it. Rotten. It was terribly unfair. This guy was too old at the time. Too insensitive. I always resented the fact that his fellow newspaper people did not do anything to prevent him from voting.

The Great Galehouse Mystery

Here it was, the next to last day of the season in 1948 and we were playing the Yankees and Joe DiMaggio. We beat them. And we beat them again the next day to eliminate the Yankees from the pennant race. When the game was over and we were sitting in the clubhouse we learned that we were tied for first place because on that afternoon Cleveland lost to Detroit. The American League pennant was to be decided in a winner-take-all playoff game in Fenway. As the Indians' train made its way toward Boston for the final game, if there

A Conversation About the

Great Galehouse Mystery

In 1948 Red Sox manager Joe McCarthy stunned Boston fans by picking the 36-year-old Denny Galehouse, who was 8–8 with a 4.00 ERA, to start the first playoff game in AL history. The Indians won 8–3 behind rookie phenom Gene Bearden. Why did McCarthy pick Galehouse? Birdie isn't telling . . . or is he?

Author: Here is a picture of Denny Galehouse.

Birdie: He's now a free-agent scout.

Author: You never told me the story of why Joe McCarthy pitched Galehouse.

Birdie: I never will.

Author: Does Ted Williams' book have it right?

Birdie: Nobody ever had it right. One of those guys said, and I don't know why, "I hope not."

Author: Who said that?

Birdie: Are you kidding?

Author: He said, "Who's going to pitch that game?" to him?

Birdie: No. I said to him.

Author: To who? Galehouse?

Birdie: No.

Author: To Joe.

Birdie: No. To someone.

Author: To someone?

Birdie: I came to such and such and said, "You may be the pitcher tomorrow." And he said, "I hope not."

Author: Does Denny know why they pitched him?

Birdie: He may have an idea, yeah. He may have an idea. I never heard him say anything. I have never said anything, so there's no need of pursuing that one. You don't indict your own teammates if there is to be an indictment, because as far as I'm concerned there is none.

Author: So? . . .

was any speculation in the clubhouse about who would pitch the all-important playoff game nobody was saying anything out loud. The Boston papers speculated that it would be either Ellis Kinder or Mel Parnell. There were arguments on both sides.

Everybody says that after we found out we were tied with Cleveland McCarthy called me into his office, which was true. But they also say that he sent me out to find out who wanted to pitch the playoff game the next day, which is not true. The conversation that we had in there was something that I just don't think I'll talk about. But there's one thing I do know. That is that Joe McCarthy didn't need somebody to give him any advice at a time like that. The story of why he picked Denny Galehouse is so logical and clear that I just don't understand why it hasn't been explained by some of these so-called expert journalists who are so completely dependent upon statistics. Stats are a great thing, but they only take you so far, and then your own logic and experience has to guide you to a decision. I will say this: I have written the reasoning of Joe McCarthy in my diaries and they are there to be read and pondered after I'm gone. If anybody cares. But his decision was so completely rational I don't understand why nobody has figured it out.

Confessions of a Pack Rat

When I was leaving Beaumont for the last time I remember packing a suitcase in the clubhouse and instinctively throwing in everything I could find: old ticket stubs, scorecards, a few balls that I begged some big-league players to sign during spring training. I even gave way to petty larceny by sneaking the Beaumont jersey out of the locker room. I decided then and there that I'd keep everything I could lay my hands on that had to do with making my way to the big leagues, because I thought that someday it might be valuable. So by the time I got near the end of my career, almost 60 years later, I had quite a haul. All kinds of junk. Old bats that had been in the World Series, old Detroit uniforms, and signed balls by the dozen.

I met Ted someplace–I forget where it was–and he had his son with him. I said, "Sign this, Ted." And it was a picture of him sliding into home plate with me blocking him. He signed it and then turned to his kid and said, "This is the toughest son-of-a-bitch I ever had to try to score on. He'd kill you." I did hurt him

The photo I had Ted sign. Boston manager Joe Cronin looks on with alarm as Ted crashes into me in a close play. Cronin gave me holy hell as Ted limped away.

on that play, and I remember it because Joe Cronin came out and gave me hell. I've got that picture hanging on my wall.

The haul was growing every year. Ma didn't have room for it at her place so I found a storage warehouse in Nashua. Then came the 1949 All-Star Game that we were to play in Brooklyn, and I was on as starting catcher. That year the Louisville Slugger people had made up two special bats for each player on each team. They were beautiful trophy bats, varnished a deep dark brownish purple mahogany with each player's name burned into every bat. They arrived in the clubhouse in a couple of big boxes, and the players all looked for theirs, swung it once or twice, tossed it aside, and went back to getting into uniform, not taking much interest in these fancy bats. The game got under way, and the first batter up was Solly Hemus. I gave the sign and wondered all the while what was going to happen to all those bats in the clubhouse. Sure as hell Joe DiMaggio wasn't going to leave the clubhouse carrying two trophy bats all the way back to Manhattan.

As the game went on I began to think that there might be a way to appropriate the useless bats in a way that would be both inconspicuous and perhaps appreciated by the people responsible for cleaning up the clubhouse. And the more I thought about it the more I felt that major league ballplayers of the quality and caliber I was playing with would have no earthly use for these fancy trophy bats that would never be swung against a curveball. And then I got an idea.

I got a single in the third inning and was standing out on first base and Yogi came in to run for me. I said, "What took you so long, Yogi?" and headed for the clubhouse with larceny in my heart. The locker room was empty except for the locker-room attendant, and as I was stripping down and before heading for the showers I handed him two $20s and a $10 and said, "I want you to gather up all these bats, put them back in the boxes, and ship them to this address in Nashua, New Hampshire." He said "OK."

Twelve years later I'm married with kids and living in Milwaukee, and I run across a guy who likes to do woodworking. We begin to talk about what to do with 50 trophy bats that have been taking up a lot of room. It took him less than a month to turn this wood into the only sofa and love seat in the entire universe made of all-star baseball bats. That's fine. The sofas are priceless, one-of-a-kind objects. Uncomfortable, but priceless. But that is not the end of the story. I'll hold that till later.

The bat theft took place in 1949, and the American League race that year was so exciting that David Halberstam wrote a book about it called *The Summer of '49.* That was the year I was leading my teammates in stolen bases, and there was nobody slower than me. Dom DiMaggio was the fastest, and he begged me to stop stealing because it was causing him some embarrassment.

Another great find came from Thurman Munson. Munson was a helluva ballplayer. He had just had a great World Series against the Dodgers, and by this time I'd become a master scout for the Yankees. As I walked through the clubhouse after the last game he was standing by his locker. I nodded a sort of congratulations to him and he laughed. He knew I was a collector and so he tore off his sweaty old batting glove and tossed it to me, and I put it away somewhere and forgot about it. But that gets ahead of the story.

Munson was doing great with the Yankees in those days, but he wanted awfully bad to be playing in Cleveland because that was near his home and family and he was developing a business relationship with a big bank out that way.

Now this is the kind of guy Steinbrenner can be. George had promised Munson he would be traded to Cleveland if ever the opportunity arose. And midseason, the very next year, with things going badly for the Yanks and with Cleveland having some pitchers who might help turn things around for New York, I was sent to Cleveland to see if a deal could be made: Munson for a couple of pitchers we wanted and some others.

I was in Cleveland for a week or so, going back and forth with Cleveland management, and late on a Thursday night I had what looked to me to be a sweet exchange. With the Yanks just finishing a series with the White Sox I flew in to Chicago to show the deal to Gabe and Steinbrenner. I checked in to the hotel and went to a favorite Chicago restaurant of mine where the owner knows me and where they leave you alone. No sooner had I been seated at my table when the owner came by to say hello and how are you and how's Mary, and he was about to move on when he turned and said, "Hey, I think I heard something just now on the radio about one of your players. In an airplane crash. I think it was Munson." I said, "Oh, no! You're kidding!" all the while knowing that the club had an off day and this was possible. The owner said to wait a minute and he went out to the kitchen. He came back a few minutes later and said, "Yes, it's your catcher, Munson. Killed in a crash of his own plane near Cleveland."

Of course it was a terrible shock. He was an extraordinary ballplayer and an awfully nice, kind, and gentle family man. And after the funeral George sent his accountants and lawyers to Cleveland to help straighten out the estate and make sure the Munson family was looked after. Something like that about George you never hear about.

Anyway, not too long ago I was going through some of the stuff in my collection, and I came across the batting glove Munson tossed me 20 years before. It was a moldy old glove. And now as I looked at it, something was wrong. I looked at it again and thought for a minute and realized it was a glove for the right hand! And Munson was a right-handed batter. Back then if you batted right, you wore the batting glove on the left hand. I figured Munson had played a joke on me, and I smiled and set it aside. Then a few days later I came across a picture of Thurman Munson at the plate, taking a swing wearing the glove on his right hand. So not only do I have the batting glove that he wore in the

Series but also proof that it was worn by the only guy who wore a glove on the wrong hand. It's what makes collecting interesting, if you happen to like the game of baseball, which I do.

Stubborn Ted

Bobby Doerr and I were sitting in the dining car on the train back to Boston after a series in Detroit when Ted came by and joined us. He had had a good series and the Detroit fans appreciated that. They were polite. Of course the fans were seldom polite in Boston, and in reprisal Ted would never acknowledge their cheers no matter how enthusiastic. He'd never tip his cap rounding the bases after hitting one into the bleachers. That was Ted. Stubborn.

But Ted would sometimes listen to Bobby, and somehow the subject came up and Bobby said, "Why don't you, for the hell of it, see what happens just once if you touch your cap?" Ted said, "To hell with them." I said, "Try it, Ted. Maybe if you do it once they won't make your life so miserable." This went on for a while and finally I got an idea. I said, "Here's what you do. You hit one out of the park. Everybody is yelling like hell. You are coming around third and just then as you reach up and touch your cap you say to yourself, 'All you bastards can go to hell,' and nobody can hear what you say, and you are happy and the fans are happy, and you live happily ever after." Bobby and I kept after him the next day and finally he said, "OK, I'll try it." Along about the seventh inning he popped one into the bleachers, and Bobby and I were standing on the dugout steps, watching as he rounded third, and his fists were clenched and we saw him mutter, "I won't do it! I won't do it! I won't do it!" And sure enough, the stubborn guy didn't do it.

Mary Hartnett Tebbetts, Baseball Wife

For a couple of years during my time with the Red Sox I would organize a few major league ballplayers into a barnstorming team. We would have promoters in some New England cities guarantee a gate, and our team of major leaguers would play a local team and divvy up the proceeds among us. It was fast money and good money, and we didn't have to work too hard to make it, and we all needed it. Vern Stephens and Jimmy Piersall and Sam Mele, all Red Sox players, were part of the team. We had one or two from the Yankees and so forth.

We ended up in Burlington, Vermont, where I was born. A nice crowd turned out for the game against a local team. We made sure our pitchers fed up fat ones for hometown favorites but we beat them anyway. After the game there was a banquet, and while I was chatting with Stephen Hartnett, a prominent citizen in Burlington, I began watching a lovely young woman with a wide smile and regal bearing chatting with someone not far away. Mr. Hartnett kept talking and I kept looking at this beautiful woman. Finally I said, "Do you know who that good-looking girl is over there? I'd sure like to meet her." And Hartnett took me by the arm, went up to the girl, and said, "Birdie, I'd like you to meet my daughter, Mary."

Mary Hartnett was at that time the secretary of Vermont's governor. She had been a WAVE in the navy during the war and had been secretary to Clark Clifford before he became President Truman's chief of staff. After the banquet I looked for her, but she had disappeared. I wondered how I was going to keep in touch with her. Then I got a letter from Stephen Hartnett, who was prominent in the Burlington Elks organization, asking what I'd charge to speak at their sports banquet that winter. I wrote back that the Elks could keep the money if I could have a date with his daughter. Mary heard about this presumptuous idea, and it took a year before she would deign to speak with me. But she finally did so and eventually said yes. Mary and I got married after the 1950 season.

Married now and with the sunset years of active play approaching, I set my sights on management opportunities, and

Red Sox general manager Joe Cronin had an idea. I was to take over management of the Triple A Birmingham, Alabama, club, and if that proved out over a year or so, I would come up and manage the Red Sox. But Joe's idea was apparently never heard by his boss, Tom Yawkey. In the middle of that winter I was awakened out of a sound sleep at 3:00 A.M. by a reporter asking me to comment on my being sold to the Cleveland Indians.

"Impossible!" I replied in shock.

I was furious and I felt betrayed. What happened was one of those outrageously unjust decisions made by capricious management that all of us who have toiled in the corporate world are familiar with. The bump in the road to my becoming a manager of a major league club began at a meeting that took place in a booth way in the back of Toots Shor's Restaurant the night before. Toots was a good friend of mine and ran this watering hole that was popular with athletes and Broadway celebrities. It was a low-lit restaurant just off Sixth Avenue on 52nd Street in New York. By that time Hank Greenberg had retired as a player and was general manager of the Cleveland Indians. As I say, he was seated in a booth at Toots' place. At the same booth was Tom Yawkey, owner of the Boston Red Sox, who also happened to own me. They were in New York for a league meeting and had started talking about a deal. It sounds crazy, but they were trying to make a deal that would trade Ted Williams to Cleveland for two of Cleveland's best pitchers. The negotiations went back and forth with Hank offering different combinations of pitchers and second stringers. All the while Yawkey backed and filled and stalled, taking on more and more Johnny Walker Black Label. The thing you have to remember about Yawkey is that he loved Ted Williams. I think he loved Ted Williams because Ted was not popular with the fans and neither was Yawkey. Fans paid good money to watch Ted play, but the Boston writers were hungry for stories and invented rumors that turned fans against him. And Yawkey didn't like me, probably because the fans seemed to like me, though they sure wouldn't spend a dime to watch me catch.

So Yawkey said to Hank something like, "I'll take Feller and Lemon and Brissie, and you get Ted Williams and a player to be named." And Hank would make a counteroffer and always ended up by saying, "And I get Ted Williams and Birdie Tebbetts." And Yawkey thought about this and offered another combination, and Hank came back and said, "And I get Ted Williams and Birdie Tebbetts." And this went back and forth with Yawkey getting madder and madder every time Hank said, "And I get Birdie Tebbetts." Finally, Yawkey got so goddamn mad hearing my name he said, "I'll tell you what, Greenberg. You want Tebbetts? Well, you can have the son-of-a-bitch. As a matter of fact, you can have him for nothing." And that's how I was sold to Cleveland for $1.

Hank and I had a good talk. We always had good talks. I loved Hank Greenberg. He was a gentleman in every sense of the word from the time I came into the big leagues. And what we talked about was, first of all, would I mind being the backup catcher for Cleveland's Jim Hegan. I said, "OK," and he said, "Because after a year I'd like you to move down to Indianapolis and manage down there and then come up and take over as manager of Cleveland." I said, "OK."

Cleveland had a young pitcher, Mike Garcia, a big burly guy. Very young. Very fast with a really good sinker. He was having a very tough time. Al Lopez was managing at the time, and he said, "Birdie, I want you to catch Garcia today and see if you can find out what's wrong."

I said, "OK" and we started the ballgame. We went through the first three innings and after he walked a guy and another got a hit in the fourth, I walked out to the mound, looked up at this big, mean-looking kid and said, "You know, God damn it, Mike. You're not trying."

"What do you mean, I'm not trying?"

"You're not trying. That's what I'm telling you." And I turned around, and all the while I'm walking back he was yelling at me. I called for the next pitch and *wham*! Here comes this fastball. I threw it back to him and called for another fastball, and he had even more zip on that one. I caught it and looked out, and he had his head hanging down. Then he looked up and nodded with a half grin. And I said, "OK." We finished that inning, and I came in and said to Lopez, "He'll be all right now."

I caught Garcia the rest of the year. I caught him 15 wins. Every once in a while he'd get a little lazy, and if I didn't pick him up right then, they could get to him.

We have a saying that when you're the defensive guy on the bench, and in the late innings of a ballgame they put you in for the regular, they call you a caddy. In other words, if a regular shortstop is playing with pain, and in the seventh inning they put in a real good defensive shortstop, the shortstop who leaves calls him his caddy: "Here comes my caddy." Well, Mike Garcia called me that. He'd walk by this weary old catcher on his last legs and say, "How ya doin', caddy? I'm keeping you in the league."

That last year I caught him and I caught Steve Gromek. I don't know whether anybody has caught as many great pitchers as I did over a whole career. I started in Detroit with Schoolboy Rowe, Tommy Bridges, and Elden Auker, and by the time I left I'd caught Bobo Newsom, Newhouser, Trucks, Trout. Then in Boston there was Mel Parnell, Ellis Kinder, and Joe Dobson. I caught all of the great Cleveland pitchers: Feller, Garcia, Early Wynn, Bob Lemon–all those Hall-of-Famers. And of course when I was a teenager I'd caught Lefty Grove.

9

"I have not failed. I've just found 10,000 ways that won't work."

–Thomas Alva Edison

Manager of the Year!

Somebody in the Cincinnati Reds front office had mentioned that *Time* magazine might be doing a piece on the Cincinnati ballclub. We were contenders, and in my second year as manager we had pulled ourselves from fifth place to second. A pennant was in sight. Attendance was up–way up–which was good for me because my salary was based partly on attendance. And then, suddenly, there it was. My face on a national magazine cover in full color and for sale for 25 cents at every newsstand in the country. Mary said it was a good likeness. She also said, "Don't let it go to your head." She didn't have to say that, because I remembered that right after DiMaggio's picture was on the cover of *Time* some bad things happened to him. A *Time* cover could be a jinx. The leap from rookie manager in the Three I League to the cover of *Time* took less than three years. Life was good, and the Tebbetts family had increased with the addition of a beautiful baby girl we named Susan.

Now, everybody thought that I was a rookie manager when I went to Indianapolis, but they forgot that I managed major league ballplayers for three years in the army. Anyway, that year in Indianapolis went well, and at the winter meeting in Chicago I heard from a friend of mine that Gabe Paul, general manager of the Reds, wanted to talk with me. But I had this

The painting used for my Time *magazine cover. Mary said, "Don't let it go to your head."*

commitment to Hank about managing the Indians when the time was right, so to honor that commitment I left orders with the hotel desk that they were to put through no calls to my room. From anybody. Well, after a couple of days this friend of mine came to me and said that Gabe wanted to talk with me but I wouldn't take his calls, and I told him that Gabe would first have to clear it with Hank. Hank said "OK," and that was the first time Gabe and I met, and it became a friendship that lasted for the next 40 years.

Anyway, we got down to business and I said, "Do you have any money?" and Gabe said, "No." What he was offering me was the same as what I was making in Indianapolis. But I wanted to manage a big-league club. So we went back and forth. At the time the attendance at the Reds games was right at 600,000, so we made a deal to the effect that I'd get an extra $1,000 for every extra 100,000 in attendance for the next year, which worked out pretty good for me because my first year with the Reds we went well over a million. Now $4,000 or $5,000 extra for a big-league manager seems like a joke nowadays, but in those days that was a lot of money.

Gabe and I, while we had our big differences, really liked each other deep down and got on just fine. Off and on. Our differences were mostly about who we were and where we came from. Gabe had been general manager of the Rochester, New York, Triple A organization and became traveling secretary of the Reds and then moved up to GM. He was and is a very straight guy. High morals. As good a man as you'd ever want. No cheating, doesn't smoke, swear, or chase women, and only on rare occasions will he take a weak drink. The trouble is that he imposed those conditions on the ballplayers. He was a Jew, but nobody knew, and he would stand by and say nothing when remarks were made about Jews. And here I was, the blue-collar Irishman with a hot temper and sometimes we would square off.

He'd yell like hell and I'd yell right back. Mostly about Gabe's insistence on imposing his morals on the ballplayers.

If there is one thing you must not do if you are a boss, a general manager, or a manager, is impose your own morals on other people. Being the boss gives you no right to judge other people. That causes problems.

I like ballplayers. I know them, how they think, how they live, and how they play after hours. Remember, I was a bachelor all the years I was playing, so I knew everything that was going on. And in my playing days I never took a drink. But I knew everything that went on, both on and off the field.

When I took over the Reds, Gabe said to me that he would not allow any beer in the clubhouse after a ballgame. Now, you've got to understand that a beer in the clubhouse after a game is a long-standing tradition in the major leagues. The guys come off the field hot, sweaty, and tired and they're wound up, whether they won or lost. Most are accustomed to a cool one on the way to the showers. So when Gabe told me that he wanted no beer in the clubhouse, I said I would announce it and tell them that the orders came from him.

Well, this went on for a while, and then we went on a road trip. We hit St. Louis and had a close, one-run loss on a hot, hot humid day. The next morning one of my players came to tell me what happened after the players left the clubhouse. Now, this was a player who was on the wagon, an alcoholic who had it under control. He said, "Birdie, you've got to do something. These guys were so wound up they went off to a saloon en masse and drank themselves silly. Then it got ugly. This ban on beer is hurting the ballclub."

I thought about this for a while and finally had an idea. I took this ballplayer to see Gabe and told him to tell Gabe what he had told me. Gabe knew this player had a struggle with booze and had gotten himself clean, and Gabe listened very carefully.

With Cleveland general manager Gabe Paul, toasting with cups of pure water. Gabe tried to impose his own strict morals on the rest of the team—a stance that caused conflicts with the players.

Finally we made a deal that this player agreed to, and I have to say I think it was a fine gesture on the part of this player. I would announce to the club that from now on players could have beer in the clubhouse after a game, but there would be one exception; this one player would not be allowed to have any. That took care of the problem.

One night when we were playing in California I was sleeping in my hotel room and there was a knock at my door. When I opened the door a couple of my players were standing there. One had a black eye and the other had a bleeding cut on his cheek. I said, "What's going on?" Now these guys were roommates! "We had a fight," they said. "We don't want to fight anymore, but we don't want to sleep in the same room."

What happened is that they had both gotten loaded and tried to make the same girl, and the struggle continued into the night. So I sent one of them back to the room and had the other one sleep in my room. But I never told Gabe what happened. One of the guys couldn't play for a few days, and we put out a story that he got out of bed in the night and hurt himself when he stumbled and fell down in the dark. They printed it, but nobody believed it. I couldn't fine them. But I never told Gabe.

I used to fine my players and not tell Gabe about it. I'd fine them $25 for an infraction that was already written out. If a guy hit a ball through the box, and in my opinion my pitcher should have fielded the ball, I'd fine him. And I think it's the greatest fault of the game today. Watch a game today and you'll see pitchers get hit in the face; you'll see the ball go through their legs. But that guy Maddux from Atlanta. The players can't hit a ball by him. Being set to field a ball is just a habit. You've got to be in the habit of being ready for a ball to be hit back to you. I can't begin to count the times a one-run ballgame was lost because a pitcher couldn't field a ball hit within his reach. If a guy on my team wasn't ready to field a ball and it got by him, I'd fine him $25. And if he complained it was $50. We had an inside kitty, a pot, and if I caught a guy out at night, rather than tell Gabe that this guy broke the curfew and have him ask what he did and who and why and who else, I'd say to the guy "$25." So if a guy was out at midnight and he was having a good time, he could take a chance on not getting caught. Nobody ever complained about that fine. And at the end of the year I gave them a party.

The other thing I couldn't tolerate was complaining about the weather. I'd fine anybody $25 for bitching that it was too hot or too cold or raining. I wanted my ballplayers to come on the field wanting to play. So this one day in Kansas City it was hotter than hell, and I was standing in the clubhouse minding my own business when I happened to hear over on the other side of the room this kid say, "Goddamn, it's hot out there!" And just when I turned to see who said it I caught the kid's eye just as he caught mine, and he sparked, "And by golly that's just the way I like it." Everybody had a good laugh over that.

The manager sets the rules that the team is going to live by. Every family has them and every team has them. They are the rules that bind them together. The manager sets the rules and sets the tone. No rules, no team. Simple as that. Of course there are always exceptions. For example, when Joe McCarthy took over as manager of the Red Sox he had a rule about dress in public off the field. Joe wanted his players dressed like gentlemen. Coats and ties. Well, Ted Williams didn't even own a tie, never wore one, and the press jumped on this, speculated on how Joe would handle it, and made a big thing about it. But Joe didn't bother. He just mumbled, "If I can't get along with a .400 hitter there's something wrong with me," then showed up in the dining room wearing a sport shirt open at the collar. Rank had its privilege.

My first day on the job as manager of the Reds, I'll never forget it. All these guys were in the clubhouse. I'd called them together to introduce myself and give them an idea of how things were going to go. As I started to talk I looked across the room and saw one guy reading a newspaper. Big Klu. Ted Kluszewski. Now this guy is our money player. A massive man. Mighty. His biceps were so enormous he had to cut off the sleeves of his jersey. If we had a star he was it. Just the year before he hit 40 home runs. And here I am, the manager, and during all my years playing in the big leagues I never hit 40 home runs. And everybody is watching to see what I'd do. Well, I did what my mother did to me when I showed bad manners. I politely said, "Mr. Kluszewski, the remarks I am making are for the whole team." Klu looked up, put the paper down, and nodded politely, having gotten the message. After that we got along fine.

I always figured that if my players liked me it was just an accident of personality. I happened to like my players, and I treated them like men. But the most important attribute of a manager is to instill confidence in his players even when they're doing badly. When a player's confidence is gone you don't have a ballplayer. I'm always curious about what will happen when I see a rookie come to bat for the first time in the major leagues. It is an indicator of what kind of ballplayer he will become.

One day we were playing an extra-inning, one-run ballgame. I was managing Cincinnati and we had two men out. They had one man on and we had a one-run lead. They sent a little left-handed hitter to pinch hit, and it was one of the years when we were in contention. The usual question comes out of the manager's mouth at a time like this. He knows he's going to get hurt if this guy hits and the question is, "Who the hell is this?" And the answer is, "Chuck Tanner."

"Anybody seen him?"

"Well, we saw him in the minor leagues." And about that time I turned around to take a look at this rookie standing in the box. Chuck Tanner in his first time at bat in the major leagues hit a home run and beat me. We became friends, and he became a great manager. But I will never ever forget the importance of Chuck Tanner because of that one time at bat, not because he was a World Championship manager.

A Dinner with Powel Crosley

I read a Cincinnati paper one morning, and a reporter had asked Reds owner Powel Crosley what was the smartest move he ever made in baseball. And Crosley said the smartest thing he'd ever done for the Reds was hiring Birdie Tebbetts as manager. Well now, that made me feel pretty good. Here's the owner of the ballclub, a multimillionaire, a bona fide genius industrialist with his name on famous brands–the Crosley radios and TVs, the Crosley cars, the Crosley washing machines. Who wouldn't feel good with a salute coming from a guy like that? I used to meet him at the ballpark where he'd shake my hand and say some polite things while the press was taking our picture together, then he'd move on, but I'd hardly call him a personal friend. He was a big man, 6'3" maybe, and well over 200 pounds.

Then this one time general manager Gabe Paul and I were invited to dine with him at the Crosley's home. His first wife had died some years before and he had divorced his second wife, so he lived alone in a big mansion up on College Hill.

We sat down in a small dining room, and he began to rave about this ham that he'd just discovered. He went on and on about this ham we were about to be served, and Gabe and I glanced at each other wondering about what was to be set before us. I was also wondering whether Gabe was going to eat the ham, although at this time I knew he was not a practicing Jew. The butler came in and put in front of each of us a small plate with a few tissues of pink flesh, sliced paper thin. Powel Crosley looked at it, took the plate in both hands, and raised it like an offering to the gods. Then he brought it down under his nose, inhaled its fragrance, and sighed in ecstasy with his eyes rolling to the ceiling. I looked at Gabe and Gabe looked at me, and finally we ate the damn ham. We got on with the rest of the meal, talking amiably about this and that. Then there was a pause in the conversation and Mr. Crosley turned to me and said, "Birdie, I want you to fire the pitching coach." Now I wasn't ready for this so I just asked why, and he said, "Because our pitching is terrible."

And I said, "That's because our pitchers are terrible. And as long as I'm manager of the Cincinnati Reds you can fire me any time you want to, but you cannot fire my pitching coach, who happens to be the very best in the business."

We went back and forth on the subject of this pitching coach, and I began to think we had been invited to dinner either to be humiliated or to be tested. And finally, feeling myself begin to lose control, I stood up, excused myself, and walked right out of the house, leaving Gabe there to deal with it. I was waiting by the car when Gabe came out a bit later, and I asked Gabe how he handled it. According to Gabe, Mr. Crosley just said meekly, "I didn't intend to make Birdie mad." And I never heard anything more about it.

Protesting

The league headquarters hate to have a game played under protest. A protest calls into question the veracity of the umpires who, after all, are in charge of the game and the enforcement of the rules. I think I won more protests than any other manager in baseball, but this one game I played under protest did overturn a rule and I'm sure that change was good for baseball.

My Cincinnati club was playing the Braves in Milwaukee. It was the top of the ninth inning and we were behind by two runs, but we had Gus Bell on second and Wally Post on first and only one out. I send Bob Borkowski up to bat for Lloyd Merriman. Warren Spahn got two strikes on Borkowski, who swung at a wild pitch that got away from the Braves catcher, Del Crandall. Borkowski took off for first. When Crandall got the ball he threw to third, trying to nail Bell, but Eddie Mathews, their third baseman, cut it off and fired across the infield. The ball hits Borkowski on the back before rolling into right field. Then Gus Bell crossed the plate and Wally Post scored all the way from first. We were tied, and I was elated.

But then the umpire, Hal Dixon, ruled both our runners out in an unassisted double play. I was mad as hell. Screaming and yelling. But the ball game was over. We argued for 20 minutes. Dixon explained that Borkowski was out automatically on the missed third strike because first and second base were occupied, and that he was invoking the penalty of calling Bell out at the plate because the batter illegally drew the throw to first.

I argued that he was crazy; that if that rule was valid, any time it was one out and a catcher had two strikes on a guy with men on base, all he had to do to make a double play was call for a pitchout, drop the ball, then when the guy moved toward first throw it into the outfield to get a double play.

We were still arguing and the stands were empty and it was getting dark, so I went into the clubhouse and called league President Warren Giles and filed a protest. He listened for a long while as I explained it a couple of times and finally said, "You're right, Birdie." Boy was I glad to hear that.

After a meeting with his umpires, Giles decided to toss out that rule, which had been on the books since Abner Doubleday. More important, he decided that we had to play that last inning over again. We did just that. Next time we Reds were to play in Chicago (a few weeks later), we took the team on a special 100-mile trip up to Milwaukee to replay just one inning. And we still lost the God damn game! But hey, I get paid for trying.

What Comes Around

There was a play at second base in Cincinnati one day that changed baseball forever. The funny thing was that it had its beginning way back in Nashua, New Hampshire, when I was a kid. It's a story that stretches over a period of about 25 years, but it shows how lasting memory can be.

When I was 11 and 12 years old I was a batboy and mascot for that team in New Hampshire, and part of that team was a baseball man named Bill Stewart. He was a part-time manger of the Nashua Millionaires. Subsequently Bill Stewart became an umpire in the National League, and later still I became a player for the Boston Red Sox in the American League. By that time, during the winter in New England, inundated by the snow and bad weather, there wasn't much you could do. But one thing that everybody enjoyed in every city and town were the sports banquets given by the Elks or Moose or some other service organization. They'd have guest speakers who might be football or basketball personnel, but mostly they were baseball people. Now these regular winter events were held in country clubs in big cities or fire stations in small towns. Occasionally I would be among that group of guest speakers and so would Bill Stewart. It was easy to get to know umpires who were speakers quite well, so between being a mascot and talking at banquets Bill Stewart and I became friendly.

Then in 1948 the Cleveland Indians were playing in the World Series against the Boston Braves. Bill Stewart was umpiring in that Series. In the first game the score was 0–0. Feller was pitching with a man on second base, and he turned and threw and picked off the runner. I think it was Phil Masi who was picked off. But Bill Stewart, who was probably thinking of something other than a pickoff by a guy like Feller, blew the play. He called Masi safe. There was no doubt that he blew the play. Right after that Tommy Holmes came up, hit a single, and the Braves went on to win the game, 1–0.

Those of us who lived in New England and played in the American League felt pretty badly about the call that Bill made. And I had to listen all that winter as he explained to banquet audiences how and why he called it right.

Ten years later I was managing the Cincinnati ballclub. There was a play at second base and Bill, who was right there, called our runner out. My ballplayer raised hell, and I ran out onto the field intending to keep my ballplayer from getting thrown out of the game and to give Bill a token complaint. He saw me coming out, and now he was going to show me, a former batboy of a team that he managed and an upstart after-dinner speaker, that he was not going to let me get away with an unfair protest. Before I got within 20 feet of him he started to blast me, and when I finally got to where he was, I said, "Bill, I walked out here to remind you of one thing: in the World Series in Boston you blew the goddamn play at second base, and now here you are again blowing a goddamn play at second base, but this time it's hurting me." And he threw me out of the game. He called me a young little–I don't know what he called me. But I was out of the game. Now, that's not an unusual story except for the fact that the next morning Lew Smith printed a column in the Cincinnati paper, quoting me and Stewart verbatim about our shouting match.

One of the unwritten rules in baseball is that when a fight is over you do not tell what you said to the umpire and he does not tell what he said to you. So the next day when I had to walk out to home plate with the lineup, Bill was there and he was furious. He thought I was the one who gave out the information, and he started to give me hell before I could explain to him that I thought he was the one who gave out the information. Warren Giles, the league president, was so damn mad about the article that he had an investigation. Here is what happened, and it changed the face of professional baseball forever. In those days photographers with those big boxy cameras were allowed to wander about the infield at will, right in the middle of the diamond. That day there had been a photographer taking a picture at second base. His name was Smitty. He was a friend of all of ours. And after he snapped a picture of the play, he stayed there while Bill and I got into this horrible argument. Now, Smitty worked for the *Inquirer*, and Lew Smith wrote for the *Inquirer*, so Smitty called up Lew and told him exactly what Bill and I had said during the confrontation, and it was printed in the newspaper. It was a helluva story. The only thing was that it made Bill and me look bad. We both thought the other guy had done it. We knew we hadn't. The end result was that when the truth came out and Warren Giles found out that the photographer had leaked this information, he banned newspaper photographers from the playing field in all National League ballparks;

it was the first time to my knowledge that had ever been done. And from that point on, from that one incident, photographers were no longer allowed on the playing field. I don't think anybody cared, because by that time they had those long-distance lenses that did the job without a photographer placing himself in a dangerous position on the field. By banning photographers Warren Giles protected executive privilege and kept the umpire and manager discourses private. Even so, most of the mistakes managers make are very public.

I'll give you a case of logic gone awry that may give some insight as to how a manager appraises a ballplayer. I had a kid named Ray Narleski at Indianapolis. Actually I had two kids. One was Don Mossi and one was Narleski. It was my first year managing. But Narleski had so much stuff I knew there was something unusual there. Mossi on the other hand had a big curve but he was a slow, lumbering kind of guy, with big ears that stuck out. In spite of that big curve he didn't show me much, so I let Mossi go. This was about halfway through the season. Narleski would pitch, and he'd have a bad time. Then he would pitch brilliantly again, a two-hitter. He'd walk right straight through all nine innings. But in three out of four times he'd pitch very well for one or two innings, and then they would romp all over him.

So I sat down and I told the secretary to get me the information on every game that Narleski pitched for me and as much as he could get on his pitching before. After studying all these stats I called up Greenberg and said, "Hank, I think we have a real great relief prospect here and his name is Narleski. I'd like to make him a relief pitcher." Hank had had trouble with that kid, contract troubles, so Hank said, "I don't care what you do with him." I said, "If he objects because he's not having a very good year as a starter, will you give him the same amount of money next year that you're giving him this year even if he doesn't make a success out of relieving?" Hank said, "Yeah, I'll do that."

So I called Narleski in and I said, "Listen. You're having a tough time as a regular and this is what I'm thinking. I'd like to put you in in the late stages of a ballgame to hold or save the game. But you have to want to do that or we won't try it. It's just one of those things." And he said, "I'm not going to do that, Birdie, damn it. When I come to arguing with that goddamn Greenberg next year he'll point out the fact that I couldn't be a starter . . ."

I said, "Greenberg knows about it."

"He'll cut my pay."

I said, "No. He's going to give you the same, at least. And if you do well, he'll probably give you more."

"I don't believe it."

I said, "Just a minute." So I got our secretary and said, "Get Greenberg on the phone." And Greenberg got on the phone and I said, "I have Narleski here. I told him that you would renew his contract right now if he wanted it or that you'd wait and see if he did well and maybe you could adjust it upwards, and he didn't believe me, Mr. Greenberg."

And Hank said, "Put the son-of-a-bitch on the phone." And Narleski got on the phone and said, "Yeah. Yeah. Yeah. Yeah . . . I don't believe you. God damn it, you . . ." I could just hear Greenberg yelling at the other end. But finally Narleski said, "Fine."

Well, we put him in as relief pitcher, and for the rest of the season the hitters had trouble getting a foul off him. And then he went to spring training and when the season opened I read in the paper about the new tandem relief pitchers that Cleveland had: Narleski and Mossi. And I said, "*Mossi*! Goddamn, Where did he come from? I let him go!" He'd become one half of "Mossi and Narleski," the two best relief pitchers of all time as a tandem.

I really blew that. But when I think of guys I made a mistake on, I think how easy it is to be swayed by flaws that hide a great talent. Maybe in Mossi's performance sheet you could find something out. Maybe he got the first guy out every time he ever came in, which is what some of these guys do. And I think that pretty much describes how and why I used to keep my own charts. I would judge a pitcher by charts. If we were winning, did he keep us winning? If we were losing, did he start us on a winning streak? Did he stop us from losing? How many games in a row did he win? I kept track of those things. I still have them. That's why after I became the executive vice president of the Milwaukee Braves I thought that, rather than the routine specifics, I needed to have a *book* on a player.

By the way, that was a time you'll never see again. While I was there a guy came in and offered us $7 million to buy the Milwaukee Braves, and we turned him down. And six days ago I picked up the paper and there's just one ballplayer signed by the Braves making $7 million a year.

I think back about the managers I've played for, some good, some bad. Take Mickey Cochrane, maybe the greatest catcher who ever played. He was a great teacher. Or Joe McCarthy. I remember one time when I was catching for the Red Sox. We were at bat with two out and ahead by a run, and it was raining pretty bad. Just before I went up to the plate I said to Joe, "Joe, do you want me to make an out?" Both of us knew that with my being the third out there was a good chance the umpire would call the game on account of rain and we'd win it then and there. And Joe said, "Birdie, I want you to go out there and try like hell to get a hit. No matter what." So I went out and I swung hard and fouled off two or three and worked up the count, and then hit a solid grounder to second and ran it out as fast as I could before I was called out. The umpire called the game in the next inning and we won it, but afterward Joe said something to me I'll never forget. He said, "Birdie, someday you'll be managing a ballgame and it will be raining like hell and one of your players will ask you if he should make an out.

And you never want to do it. You never know when the Good Lord is going to stop the rain. And you never want the umpires to pass the word around among themselves that you aren't always playing as best you can. That way you'll always have their respect."

It was only five years later in Indianapolis that the same situation arose. Raining like hell, and two men out. We were ahead

Praying for rain. It was Joe McCarthy who taught me to always play as hard as I could—even in bad conditions—because you don't want word to get out amongst the umpires that you aren't always giving it your best shot. That way, he said, "You'll always have their respect."

by one run and the game had just become official when the batter whispered to me, "Birdie, you want me to make an out?" I said, "Hell, no. Hit the son-of-a-bitch out of the park." And he did. And the sky cleared. And the other team pulled ahead and beat us in nine innings. I'd have given anything to hear what those umpires said to each other when that ballgame was over.

Mighty Casey

I used to feud with Casey Stengel around home plate on occasion. We would scream back and forth. Anyway, Casey and I were not on a very friendly basis, I thought, because of a close play at the plate in Yankee Stadium one day. But after I became manager of Cleveland I walked into Toots Shor's in New York, and Casey was sitting in what they called the quiet corner where guys like managers and people like that were seated. I went down there because he motioned for me to come, and I sat with him and we visited.

I once said about Casey Stengel that if I owned his oil wells I wouldn't finish my sentences either. Casey's speech is hard to track, but it is interesting to try. Soon Toots came by to insult us for a while, and Casey looked up at Toots and said, "Let me tell you about this feller." And he started describing a play when I was catching for the Red Sox against the Yankees. "And our feller led off with a double and gets over to third, and the tall guy hit a bouncer to the feller out there with the arm, and he throws beeline to this here one who just stands there not noticing the ball is going to hit him on the head so the guy coming in from third thinks he don't have to slide, but he does have to slide because this here feller has been faking not caring until the last second when he grabs the ball and tags my guy out with this bush play in front of the whole goddamn world. Smart feller here."

Toots wandered off to insult somebody else, and I reminded Casey that his Yankees went on to beat us in the final game of that year and that I was the guy who made the final out and that Tommy

Henrich, who I'd tagged out on that bush play, made my final out. We had fun talking that night, and I was amazed that he was so friendly. Finally I couldn't hold it in any longer and said, "Casey how do you do it?" He looked at me as if he didn't understand. So I said it again. "How do you do it?" And he wrinkled up that ugly face until he figured out what I was asking and said–and this story has been printed, but it hasn't been printed the way it happened–he said, "Birdie, I never play a game without my man in the lineup." Then he waited and took a sip of his bourbon. In the pause I'm thinking he's talking about DiMaggio, he's talking about Mantle, he's talking about this guy and that guy, and suddenly I realize he's talking about Yogi Berra. Yogi would be in left field, or he would be at first base, or he'd be behind the plate, and I wouldn't be surprised if somebody didn't tell me at one time Casey didn't put him in at third. But he never played a ballgame without Yogi, including a World Series where once he really did put the man in left field. And that meant to me that, one, Casey knew what his players could do and, two, he knew how to instill confidence in his players to do what was needed to win. Old Casey would have a great time now with the designated hitter as part of the game.

That's a great thing, that designated hitter thing. I'm being ironic. These owners cry about money and then they put a designated hitter on, and that adds a half a million, maybe a million dollars to their payroll for a ballplayer that probably can't play. And then they squawk about losing money. How would you like to play every day and see a guy making a million dollars just to sit on the bench?

Swell-Headed Stars

When Joe McCarthy came to manage the Red Sox, the newspaper boys had a lot of fun speculating about how he would handle Ted Williams–because the relationship between a big star and a manager who is making only a fraction of the other guy's money can be troublesome. I had to deal with something like that in the case of a Cleveland player named Rocky Colavito. He was making about $60,000 or $70,000. That was a lot of money in those days, and certainly more money than I was making as manager. He was a classy outfielder. Power at bat. No question a great asset to the ballclub.

This one day in Cleveland, late in the second half of a doubleheader with the Yankees, there was a man on first and a guy hit a fly ball to Colavito. He fielded it on the first bounce. The runner on first went on to second and then way past the bag, but Colavito held the ball in his hand and started playing cat and mouse with the guy, teasing him. Then suddenly the runner took off for third and Rocky, in a panic, threw the God damn ball into the stands.

I watched this from the bench and, hard as it was, I maintained my composure. A manager must never berate a player in front of fans. That is done in private. It is also important that the roving, probing television camera never catch a manager off guard or with a downcast expression. Anyway, we lost the ball game and I didn't say anything in the dugout, but still I was madder than hell.

Well, when I got to my office I asked the clubhouse boy to tell Colavito to come see me right away. The kid came back a minute later and, putting a polite spin on it, this is what he said: " Birdie, Rocky says for you to stuff it." Wow! I walked out of the office madder than hell and I went right up to him and I said, " Listen, Colavito, when I want to talk with you in my office I want you to respond. Promptly. $500!"

Well, when Gabe Paul heard the story he said, " Birdie, you know that any fine over $250 has to be cleared by the commissioner. I think you ought to back off." I said, "I'm not backing off. It's him or me, Gabe."

It got to be pretty dicey, because Rocky called the head of the Major League Players Association. Now this guy was Judge Bob

Cannon, a neighbor and very dear friend of mine from my days in Milwaukee, and I knew this put him in a tough spot. So what the hell do you do? We were going into New York in five days or so, and Judge Cannon and Rocky were going to hold a hearing with Commissioner Ford Frick when we got there. So I called Mr. Frick and told him what was happening. I told him that he could do whatever he wanted, but that I was not going to appear with Colavito and Cannon and argue the case.

I heard they showed up and Frick stuck by me, but Cannon was madder than hell, and when he got back to the hotel I met him in the foyer with a big grin and offered to buy him coffee. He told me to stuff it and asked what time the players' bus to Yankee Stadium was going to leave because he wanted to ride with them. I told him it left promptly at 5:00, which was a lie, but I wanted to fix his ass. The bus was actually supposed to leave at 4:30.

So at about 4:45 the entire Cleveland ballclub was sitting on the bus, the door closed, and out of the Biltmore Hotel walked the Honorable Judge Robert Cannon, Esquire, looking this way and that. He came up and rapped on the door of the bus. I was sitting in the first seat, where the manager sits. I let him knock a few times, then finally I told the driver to open up. Cannon got on and I looked at him and yelled for everybody to hear: "Who the hell do you think you are that you can keep the entire ballclub waiting a half an hour while you're sound asleep upstairs? " And he said, "You told me the bus left at 5:00." And I said, "Come on, Cannon. Sit here with me." And he yelled out as loud as he could, "Tebbetts, I wouldn't sit beside you if I had to walk all the way to Yankee Stadium!" I had to have the last laugh.

Clubhousing

The one thing that disturbs me, and I don't know if it's because of the way I was brought up in baseball, but when I was out there managing from the bench and there was a baseball game going on, I used to turn around and say to someone who was sitting next to me, "What's the count? What's the score? What is so and so? How many outs?" And the guys that were on the bench would have their heads in the ballgame. They had to answer a question that I would ask them, and the end result was that so many times during the course of a career a ballplayer would come up and say, "I think I've got their hit-and-run sign." Now he's sitting on the bench, nothing to do, and he's watching the game. He's a player and he comes over and says, "I think I've got the hit-and-run." That can make a difference. Nowadays if you walk into the dressing room of a ballclub while a game is going on, even if it's for a national championship, you might see two or three ballplayers having a cigarette or for all I know maybe playing cards. During the course of a game! And the television is on. I think they don't care. Those are things that come along and you see change happening, and it makes you wonder. They're new people and that's the way it's done today, but it's hard for a guy like me to accept. They claim that when they go back to the clubhouse they can see what a pitcher is doing on TV and what he's throwing and everything else. I don't think that's true. It might be true if you're working in a factory and you go off at quitting time and leave things to the night shift–everything is routine in a factory. But in a ballgame the situation changes with every pitch, and even sitting on the bench a guy can somehow make a contribution.

Ted's Favors

Ted Williams, after his playing days, was the supreme instructor of hitting for the Red Sox during spring training. Every springtime when I managed Cincinnati, if I had a young player of great promise coming along and we were going to play the Red Sox, I would catch Ted's eye and say, "Are you ready, Ted?" And he would say, "Yes, send him over." I would send my young players who I thought were going to be great hitters over to talk to this great man. So I would send Frankie Robinson over and I would send Ed Bailey over. I didn't send green kids over. Maybe there were about three. I remember more than anybody else sending Frankie Robinson. And Ted would take these players out in the outfield and give them a lesson. Williams would just stand there with a bat and talk to them. He had never seen them before and he would never see them again, but he would talk to them. He would tell them what he hit, how he hit, and how he did this and that. He had been my teammate on the Boston Red Sox, and now I was manager of Cincinnati, and these were Cincinnati players who were friends of mine. I would say to them, "Tell Ted you want to talk with him and I said so." Ted would give a clinic, and they were all in of awe of this guy. Doing something like that was unheard of. And that's what you call a helluva favor.

Radical Remedies

When you're a manager of a baseball club, sometimes you will go up against a great hitter who you just can't get out. I'm thinking now of a DiMaggio or a Musial or a Williams in a tight game with men on base. In that situation sometimes your pitcher needs special help. Mickey Cochrane once told me that if anybody hits you to a point where you just feel as though you can't get him out, that means that he's thinking with you. He has cracked your code. Therefore, you've got to do something about that chain of thought. The thing to do to break that chain is to tell the batter exactly what the next pitch is going to be. First be sure that you and the batter and the manager and the umpire understand what is going on, and then and only then should you throw the pitch. This strategy destroys the concentration that the batter had, because it is an unbelievable thing for a pitcher to tell you, "I'm going to throw you a fastball." It makes it difficult for you to be ready to hit the fastball because it puts that little doubt in the batter's mind that is very effective when you're pitching against a guy who seems to bat

.400 or .500 against you. You don't use this strategy against somebody you have no problem with. It should be used against that one hitter who has figured out your thought pattern.

Over my lifetime we tried that trick maybe 10 times. One of those times was with Ted Williams when I was catching for Detroit. Ted will tell you about it. Bill McGowan was umpiring at the time, and I forget who the pitcher was, but I was catching, and along about the sixth inning Ted came up to the plate. He'd already gotten a couple of extra-base hits, and as he stepped in I went down and said, "We're going to throw you a fastball, Ted." And it was a fastball, and he took it for strike one. And then I said, "Another fastball, Ted." It was, and McGowan yelled, "Strike two!" I said "Curveball, Ted." And when the curve floated in, he swung and dribbled it in front of the mound and was thrown out. Next time up we did the same thing. "We're giving you a curveball, Ted." It sailed in, and he swung and missed. "Fastball, Ted." And he took it for a strike. By now he was really mad, and I said, "Another fastball, Ted," and it was a fastball, and he gave a half swing and McGowan called him out. He turned to McGowan and said, "This son-of-a-bitch is throwing the game. He's telling me every goddamn pitch." And old Bill just grinned through his mask and said. "Yes, Mr. Williams. Looks like he's got you psychoanalyzed."

We also tried it in Milwaukee. One of our better pitchers was having trouble with Orlando Cepeda, so we said, "OK, we'll tell Cepeda what's coming, and he can't hurt us any worse than he has." And so we did. Unbelievably he took two more strikes and looked around as though we were cheating. He was confused. We had luck with him. About his third time at bat we told him what was coming, but the pitcher decided to throw a curveball instead of a fastball, and when he did that, Cepeda no longer was fooled. He just got up there and went back to the way it was before, with no doubts. It's a risky way of getting a hitter out, but it can be effective if you have the guts to do it.

Another effective defensive move was introduced to me by Lou Boudreau. When Boudreau used to manage the Indians he would often have his infielders shift to the right when Ted Williams was at bat, leaving third base wide open, because Ted rarely hit to the left. He could if he wanted to, but that was not often his choice. The shift was daring and it didn't slow Ted down much. However, I tried that shift once when I managed Cincinnati. One of our pitchers was having trouble with Musial, and it really upset him. I put the shortstop deep into right field. Musial complained to the umpire, but there was nothing he could do about it. As I remember he popped up to the infield.

Off the Field

A manager's job doesn't end when the last man is out. One difficult moment for me came up a few days after we got back from a long road trip. One of my best pitchers came into my office after a game, closed the door, and sat down. Almost in tears he said, "Birdie, I think I've got a problem." I said, "What's the matter?"

Now this kid has been married a couple of years to a lovely wife, and they are talking about having a family, and he's got a bright future in baseball once he gets a little more control over his slider. He says, "I was out late one night in St. Louis and met this girl in a bar . . ." and before he could finish I told him to stand up and drop his pants and show it to me, and sure enough he had a dose. And to make matters worse he had come home and exposed his wife.

I've long forgotten what words the team doctor used to induce the guy's wife to surrender without questioning to being punctured by a hypodermic, but I do remember that this pitcher came back a week later and threw a four-hit shutout.

That brings up the whole question of wives and families of ballplayers. We don't spend enough time counseling the wives in baseball, because the people up in the skyboxes don't realize that a player is not just a talent, that he has a life outside of baseball–a wife, kids, and all the rest. We have to pay more attention to that. The family life of everybody is terribly important, but when you work as closely together as baseball players then the rest of life becomes the responsibility of the women. And Mary was wonderful at that.

I had one guy play for me whose wife went to bed and didn't get up again for months.

There are so many things–and you can't blame the wives for it–but there are so many things that happen on the field and in the dugout that are the result of grudges and misunderstandings among the wives. "I don't like your wife, my wife doesn't like your wife, but I like you, and you and I are getting along great. But it's hard for us to beat this thing down when we're in the same ballpark and playing the same game, and they're sitting close together watching us from the stands." And if you're the manager, you know something is wrong but you don't know what it is. But you better look deep because at the end of the day it is going to affect the outcome of a game. I had a priest who helped me in this area. He traveled all over the country. He was a "redemptive priest," and he was very friendly with a couple of the owners. Catholic or Protestant or born-again Christian, when a player was having problems and I finally found out that they were marital problems, I brought him in. Paid him out of my own pocket. He straightened out marriages and straightened out differences. And, as I say, it was a nonsectarian type thing. He was a very good friend of my wife's, which is how I met him.

When I managed the Braves in Milwaukee there was a horrible feud between Warren Spahn's wife and Lew Burdette's wife. I was aware of it. One of them didn't want them to room together on the road.

There was also a feud between Mrs. Burdette and me. An unforgiving thing. And it was her own grudge. He didn't bear it, but he could only be as nice as he could be when she wasn't around. When she was around he had to hold back.

Lou Gehrig and Babe Ruth had a severe falling out and didn't speak to each other for years because of their wives, as I understand it. It affected the relationship between those two guys on the field. A manager has to have an understanding of that. I don't know whether a manager today can get that close to a player anymore. Nowadays a player is so rich he's a private corporation. You ride the players' bus to the ballpark nowadays, and you will see a shortstop getting on carrying *The Wall Street Journal* and you'll hear these young guys talking about their portfolio. Not like in my day!

I like baseball players. I played the game all my life. I understand. I was single until I was 40, and I knew what was going on. I was always out on the town. And nothing could happen in the off hours that I didn't know about, whether a guy was married or single, because I was always out after hours.

The baseball player's life is great for the men, but it's tough on the women and even tougher on the kids. A ballplayer packs his bags and says "so long" to the lady, tells her to look after the kids, and he's gone. And the next thing he knows the kids are in school and graduating, and where has he been? Somewhere along the line he has to get to know his kids if they are going to turn out OK.

Fast-Changing Times

Anybody who thought about such things would ask themselves, Why didn't I think of that? Night baseball in the forties changed the game, and here it was in the fifties and two new technologies were going to change it again. The first was the jet plane, which would make it possible to fly a ballclub across the country in five hours instead of twelve. The second was cable television, which could bring a hundred channels into every home, so that a guy living in a trailer in Podunk could watch the Yankees play the Angels or any other combination you could think of. Another big change was legal. We have Curt Flood to thank for that. Where the hell was Curt when we needed him? He of course broke apart the reserve clause and freed players from those lifetime indentured contracts and, along with the advent of cable television, made millionaires out of journeymen ballplayers. Am I envious? Yes, indeed!

When I got my contract to manage Cincinnati for the 1958 season, something was missing. There was no provision in it for an attendance bonus. That was very important to me because it meant I would get more money if attendance was over 600,000. Mary and I had a growing family, a mortgage on a house in Nashua, and two cars, and we needed the bonus. I interpreted the missing attendance bonus as a sign that Powel Crosley was going to move the Cincinnati franchise to the empty Polo Grounds in New York. The jet age made possible the New York Giants' move to San Francisco and the Brooklyn Dodgers' to Los Angeles. If the Cincinnati franchise moved to New York's Polo Grounds, attendance would go through the roof. At least that's the way I read the tea leaves. But if that was the plan, it never got off the ground. Gabe Paul took the job of general manager of the Houston expansion team, and during spring training Crosley died. Things went badly for the club that year, and I resigned as manager of the Cincinnati Reds in midseason, turning the reins over to Jimmy Dykes. I started looking for a new job.

10

"I've had a wonderful time, but this wasn't it."

–Groucho Marx

The Big Shot

I found a job, but it was different from any job I'd ever had. Lou Perini, a highly successful operator in the construction business in Boston, had bought controlling interest in the Boston Braves and moved the franchise to Milwaukee. After some stunning successes in the early years, the franchise was in decline, and Lou asked me as a friend from New England to move my family to Milwaukee to help protect his investment. Mary and the kids and I rented a house in a town called Wauwatosa on the outskirts of Milwaukee and settled in. I became a big shot. The job required that I wear a coat and tie and a snap-brim fedora. It also required that I sit in long boring meetings and discuss the Blue Cross/Blue Shield contract for groundskeepers and the price to charge for hot dogs. It required that I read without understanding the contract for the rental of County Stadium and that I knew which contractors were going to bid on paving the parking lot. I was now a baseball executive. I hated it, but with three kids and another on the way I needed the job. One day I found myself sitting all alone in the stands out in

Susan Tebbetts Mitchell on

Life with Birdie

Mom brought us all in a room and said, "We're having a family meeting." Now remember, I'm in the fourth grade, nine years old. She asked everybody, "Is it OK with everybody in the family if Dad goes back into a uniform and manages in the dugout and is on the field? It will mean less money for our family." Why did he do that? Why did he do that? I'm the oldest and I'm in the fourth grade. And we all said, "Oh no, we don't care. No, Dad, fine." So he went back into uniform. Then we got robbed several times in Wauwatosa, outside of Milwaukee, since he was manager of the Braves and thieves knew when he was on the road. And of course during spring training the house would be empty and the whole family would be gone.

right field. I had a pair of field glasses, and although a ballgame was going on I was not watching the game, much as I wanted to. Instead, my field glasses were pointed on some gamblers in the left-field stands betting on the game. I had the security guys kick them out of the park.

One of the perks of the job was working alongside a young guy named Roland Hemond, who was learning the baseball management trade. Roland was just one of the people I met during my Milwaukee days who would become a lifelong friend. Another was Judge Robert Cannon, who not only presided in court on the bench in Milwaukee but was also the Major League Baseball Players representative.

Chuck Dressen was managing the Braves club at the time, and things were going badly for him. There came a time in mid-summer when Lou Perini happened to catch me at the ballpark looking wistfully toward the pitcher's mound at a left-hander who should have been pulled before any more damage was done. A day or so later I was no longer executive vice president wearing a coat and tie but manager of the Milwaukee Braves wearing flannel knickers, which suited me just fine. And Perini was happy because I was off the executive payroll.

How Mary and the kids were going to take the news was a worry because I had to take a cut in pay. And by this time my three daughters were becoming people with hopes and dreams and personalities of their own that needed, indeed demanded, attention. Sue was the oldest. Then came Betty and Pat. George Jr. was an infant, redheaded and going through his terrible twos. To watch him scamper among the furniture I saw a future shortstop.

One of the consequences of being a manager of a ballclub turned out to be that the whole world knew when you were out of town. Of course the only people who seemed to care were thieves. After having our house robbed a couple of times Mary and I started thinking about finding a solution to the problem.

Hutch

By the time I became a manager in the major leagues, that kid Fred Hutchinson had been managing for a few years, first in Detroit and later in St. Louis. During the war he had gone into the service, as most of us did, and after the war he picked up where he left off, always with Detroit. By now he was married and living someplace in Florida, and whenever I'd run into him he'd try to sell me on the idea of moving from New Hampshire down to this place he called Anna Maria Island. Hutch had a first-rate baseball mind, and while he'd made it as manager, all he had really ever wanted was to win 20 games and beat me on the golf links. We played whenever we could during spring training. While chasing the golf ball he'd try to get me to buy a home in Florida.

Once Hutch invited me over to his house to meet his wife, Pat, and to see his new baby. Hutch and I were good friends. Close friends. We went way back and had fought a lot of battles together. And we always leveled with each other. Even when we were kidding we were honest. So Hutch picked this little bundle out of the crib and held it up to me to look at and I looked at it. And I laughed. And I said, "Hutch. That's the ugliest-looking baby

Susan Tebbetts Mitchell on

Life with Birdie

When we moved to the island from Milwaukee (none of us knows the reason why–my guess would be winters off in nice weather), we initially rented a beautiful home, and Dad and Mom wanted desperately to purchase the home across the street from it on Beach Avenue. That house was designed like a brick castle, turret included. It was owned by Earl Torgeson's wife, Norma (Earl was a divorced ballplayer). Dad loved the house and was willing to wait until Norma was ready to sell. During one spring when Mom and Dad were out of town, they found out that Norma sold the home one night over drinks without calling them, and they were crushed. Shortly after that they purchased the house at 229 Oak Avenue, along with the lots on either side. At the time, the street was undeveloped. Mom was concerned about storms and water levels. She wanted the home in the town of Anna Maria because that was the widest part of the Island. We had the benefit of the canal for a boat to get to the bay. We could walk to the beach to swim in the Gulf. But during hurricanes, she felt we had a good chance of ending the storm with an undamaged building on that street. I think they had big renovation plans when they purchased the house, but it didn't work out.

I ever saw." And Pat threw me right out of the house. But she got over it, after I apologized.

With winter coming on and the thought of deep snow on one hand and waving palms on the other I talked Mary into trying a winter in the sun in Florida. We rented a house on Anna Maria Island.

Toward the end of the season Mary took the kids to Florida in time to start school, leaving me alone in the big house in Wauwatosa. There were so many wonderful, wonderful eating places in Wauwatosa. Neighborhood restaurants. There was one particular restaurant and bar I liked, and I would go there after games. I got to be known there and finally got to sit with the same guy every night. We would drink and visit. He was a brilliant guy.

And as the evening wore on, his wife would leave us, with a shake of her head. At the end of the night he would say, "Birdie, one more." And I would say, "Gus, I'm with you." Now, he lived in a house a block from the bar and I lived about two and a half or three blocks away. He could get home and I would get home somehow. Luckily the restaurant had some wonderful waiters and waitresses who didn't mind a little exercise at night, and they would steer me in the right direction, and I would somehow make it. I loved that restaurant. And I loved the guy and his wife who I visited with there. He had a son who played baseball. I told Gus that his son was a good major league ballplayer and that it was too bad the young man was in the minor leagues. He kept telling me that the boy should be playing for the Milwaukee ballclub. Moreover, he said that we didn't know what we were doing, and he called me "an Irisher." His name was Uecker, Bob Uecker's father.

I went into the restaurant one night and told Gus, "We are going to bring up Bob tomorrow. He's coming up from Louisville." And Gus said, "What's the difference. He comes up, he sits down on the bench, and you don't hear anything about him. You don't give him a chance." And I thought, "Well, he's probably right. We've got the best catcher in the National League, the No. 1 catcher in Del Crandall, and Bob is probably going to come up and not catch." So I said, "I'll tell you what I'll do, Gus. Tomorrow night I will catch your son, Bob Uecker." And he said, "You better, you Irisher so-and-so. If you don't I'll never speak to you again."

The word got around in the restaurant that Bob was going to catch, and that night and the next morning the restaurant owner called everyone he knew who was a customer of his and said that they were going to have one or two buses leaving from the restaurant and going down to the ballpark. He also told them that Birdie had arranged for them to have excellent seats and that Bob Uecker was going to make his major league debut. Uecker was going to catch, and anybody who went to the game on the bus and came back to the restaurant was a guest of the saloon. They had a mob down there at that ballgame. The ballplayers were announced as they usually are, and as the crowd was applauding and the ballplayers ran out onto the field, Bob Uecker strolled out onto the field, got to home plate, and stopped. He turned and faced the crowd, threw his hands up in the air as though he had just won the Olympics, and bowed gracefully and humbly toward the stands. And that gang from the restaurant made more goddamn noise than the other 25,000 people in the ballpark. I really believe that was one of the highlights of the year.

Patricia Tebbetts Kirton on

Life with Birdie

He used to write letters to us when he was on the road. He would take a legal pad and he'd be on a plane or in a motel or hotel, and he'd write, "Dear Mommy, Betty, Sue, George, and Sis," and then he would write the whole letter. And then he would sign it, "Love, Birdie, Bird, George," so it was an appropriate signature for each one of us. Then, when he got back home, he gave Mom all of these letters and asked her to Xerox them and mail them out to everybody. So every six months or so, I would get about 30 letters from Dad all at one time. He never put anything in the mail. And he never wrote a letter to any of us individually, just everybody as the whole gang. That's Birdie.

Bob was a good ballplayer. He could throw. He couldn't hit a curveball, but some guys couldn't throw the curveball over so he could spot the curve and go for the fastball. I thought he was one of the most underrated ballplayers in the major leagues. As a matter of fact, I thought we had another exceptionally underrated ballplayer in our catching staff as well. And that was Joe Torre, who had to watch the very well established Del Crandall, who had proved his value by being a World Series winner. So it was a very difficult thing to be a Milwaukee catcher. I want to salute Bob and tell you he was a very good major league ballplayer.

The other folks Mary and I became friendly with were the Cannons, Judge Bob Cannon and his wife. As the players representative for the Major League Players Association he was a natural choice to become baseball commissioner, but he lost out on that assignment by just one vote. He would have been a great commissioner. Feeling lonely, I would sometimes walk in through the back door of their house seeking company and baseball talk. Bob and I were deep in conversation one night (and by the way, this was long before the Colavito episode) when we realized that I had only one cigarette in my pack and the judge had only two in his. An hour later we were out of smokes and began to get kind of nervous, so we swore an oath to each other that we would give up cigarettes forever. So help us God! On the way home that night I stopped off at the drugstore to pick up a pack of Chesterfields and decided to buy two packs, one for me and the other for Judge Cannon, who was deeply grateful to me for bringing them by before he went to bed.

Then on a sunny winter day in Florida, just after Mary got the kids off to school and as I was heading out the door with Hutch to play a couple of rounds of golf, word came in. Lou Perini had sold the Braves and the franchise would be moved to Atlanta. Jobless again.

One of the amazing things about the baseball business is that while the games go on above ground, the earth is always trembling underneath. No matter which baseball club I was working for, all the while there was the possibility that in some boardroom far from home plate a bunch of millionaires would be plotting to sell a club to another millionaire or a syndicate or move a franchise from this city to that one. Then my old friend Gabe Paul, after a bellyful of Texas pointy-toed politics with the Houston Astros, put together a syndicate to buy the Cleveland Indians. Guess who he chose to be manager? Gabe and I together again. Hot dog!

Susan Tebbetts Mitchell on

Life with Birdie

It was Mom that said, "By God, if these kids are gonna pay the price of having a baseball life, they're gonna get the benefit." Dad very willingly set us up and said, "Have a blast. You're gonna stay in this nice hotel. And you're gonna get the pool, and you're gonna get the tennis, and you're gonna get whatever it is you want."

At last, Mary and our big family were beginning to get the best of both worlds: the income and excitement of big-league summers in Ohio and the warm, sunny winter days on Anna Maria Island, where my kids could grow up in a friendly small-town atmosphere. And Freddie Hutchinson and I could play golf every winter day. And we did. For just one winter.

It was Mary's idea to pull the kids out of school and take them to the Indians spring training camp in Tucson. That was OK by me. The baseball wife's life is not an easy one, and if that made the family life somehow better, I was all for it. My only worry had to do with the problems that arise with all children of people whose names are in the papers. I had seen the damage to ballplayers' kids who were showered with unearned attention. So I wanted my kids to have a happy childhood and at the same time have the chance to grow up just as other kids do.

Gabe started me off with a big press conference in downtown Cleveland, and I tried to exude confidence and optimism. I looked over the Cleveland roster and noted that the great Cleveland pitching tradition of the likes of Feller and Lemon and Garcia was long gone. But across the American League the managers I'd be up against were all old friends. Ralph Houk was running the Yankees, Al Lopez in Chicago, Sam Mele in Minnesota, Billy Hitchcock in Baltimore, and Johnny Pesky in Boston. Except for Whitey Ford, who won 24 that year (1963), it was not a great era for pitching.

I made a terrible mistake during a game in Baltimore, and a very good friend of mine was a casualty of the mistake. He did not take advantage of my mistake and that cost him dearly. We were playing the Orioles and I had a left-handed pitcher warming up in the bullpen. It looked as though it was no contest; we had it under control. But in the ninth inning Baltimore's first hitter got on. Then came a base on balls and I was upset. I didn't like it even though there were two men out. I ran out to the mound and said, "That's all!" and waved in Allen, my left-handed pitcher. He came in and was announced. The umpire was about 15 feet from me when I told him that this was my pitcher.

Now, we had a two-run lead and two men out. I told my pitcher, "I want you to make this guy hit a curveball, and if he hits anything it's not going to hurt you. You've got enough lead, so get the ball over the plate. I prefer a curveball." He said, "Yes, sir." As he said that I turned and

Patricia Tebbetts Kirton on

Life with Birdie

Every spring when he was manager of the Indians, we'd pack up and move to Tucson for spring training. For at least one month the whole family would go to spring training. We had a tutor. He came to the hotel where everybody stayed, and we studied for half the day, and for the rest of the day we had time off. We just hung out, having a good time, walking around and seeing all the ballplayers lounging about the hotel.

Dad and Mom had an adjoining room with ours, so you could open the door and see them. They would tell the people in the hotel, "These are our kids. Let them charge their food. Give them free reign. We are responsible for anything that they do." And then they would tell us, "You better respect everybody in this hotel, and you better be great kids." By then I was in seventh grade and we had our own little kitchen, our own rooms, and a little choo-choo train that would come by and pick us up and take us over to the pool and to the spring training games.

Patricia Tebbetts Kirton on

Life with Birdie

Mom used to pick us up from elementary school when Dad managed the Cleveland Indians–throw us all in the back of the station wagon–and she would drive up from Florida to Cleveland with us. Dad, of course, flew up. Mom drove with four kids from Anna Maria Island to Cleveland. I don't know how she did it. That's a lot. Four kids in a station wagon, driving to Cleveland.

Susan Tebbetts Mitchell on

Life with Birdie

At every little old podunk Ramada Inn, Mom would walk right up to the front desk. She'd say, "I'm Mrs. Birdie Tebbetts." Of course, they'd recognize the name. She'd say, "We'll be checking in, and my children will be eating in your restaurant. Let them run up a tab. Whatever they want, give them. They'll be very polite. Please help them out." And she'd go to her room, and I would think to myself, "She is something. She's a force." Now I finally realize why she went up to the front desk rattling her gold bracelets and gold charms.

took a close look at him. I couldn't believe it. He was half in the bag. Drunk. I walked off the rubber and gave the sign to Coach Tom Ferrick out in the bullpen to have somebody ready, and he gave me the OK. Then Allen threw a curveball in the dirt. I was fuming. The next pitch he threw was a curveball that went halfway to home plate. By then I was so angry that I went out there and told him to get the hell off the field. "Get the hell out of the ballpark." And I waved to Ferrick to send me a pitcher. And Ferrick was trying to tell me that his pitcher wasn't ready. And I told Ferrick I didn't care whether he was ready or not.

I turned to the umpire and said, "So-and-so is coming in to replace my pitcher." And the umpire said, "Yes, sir!" In went my new pitcher and Ferrick was screaming at me from the bullpen, and who the hell can hear him? By then the new guy had been announced as the pitcher, but

Ferrick finally got me on the phone and said, "Allen has got to pitch to one hitter and have the hitter complete his time at bat or else he's an illegal pitcher and we're apt to lose the ballgame." At that point Allen was in the clubhouse and the new guy was warming up on the mound, about to throw a pitch. I looked over at the Baltimore dugout, and Bill Hitchcock was having a conference with his coaches, who were aware that Allen did not pitch to one hitter for his time at bat. The umpire said, "Play ball," and my relief pitcher threw a strike. Then Hitchcock called time out and walked up to the plate, and I could just see my boss, Gabe Paul, listening to this ballgame on the radio and calling me every kind of a dumb son-of-a-bitch that ever lived. And he was going to be right. It was too late. There was nothing I could do about it. So I walked up to home plate to listen in on my own crucifixion just as the umpire was saying to Hitch, "When this pitcher was announced, Billy, he became illegal, and you had to come out at that time to declare him an illegal pitcher and to have the pitcher who was the legal pitcher complete pitching to the hitter. When you allowed the relief pitcher to throw one pitch, you then accepted the fact that he was now legal, and you have no possibility of complaint." And I turned around and walked into the dugout, and thought to myself, "I'm going right in the clubhouse to see Mr. Allen." I walked into the clubhouse with murder in my heart and lucky for him, Allen had dressed without showering and left the ballpark. If Hitchcock had complained right away, I might have had to go find Allen in a saloon in downtown Baltimore to pitch to the batter.

So no matter what, I screwed up. Everybody screwed up, and I got away with the infraction, and I didn't get fired. I felt stupid and sorry for Bill Hitchcock because they gave him hell the next day for not knowing the rule. I did not get the blast that I deserved. The umpire at any time could have indicated when I took Allen out of the game that he had not completed pitching to the hitter. But he chose not to do that. I brought the guy in, he was announced, and he threw a ball. The umpire was not responsible for the violation. I was. That was the dumbest thing I ever did in all of my managing career. At least, it was the dumbest thing that I know about.

Fredrick Charles Hutchinson, 1919–1964

Pat Hutchinson told Mary and Mary told me. Hutch had discovered a bump on his neck and called his brother, a well-known doctor in Seattle. And Fred's brother said, "Get your ass out here right away." And he did. Melanoma. Cancer. It quickly metastasized, giving him bumps on his head. Not readily curable. Chemotherapy. Intense. That winter no golf. I drove over to his hospital in Bradenton every day, and we talked. And every so often he would get violently ill. And Hutch, in pain, would say, "Birdie, press my head. Press my head." And I tried. I did press his head. I tried like hell. And finally I broke down and said to his wife, Pat, "I can't do it anymore. I just can't handle it." But I came back to see him every day, and we talked. Within a year Hutch was gone. And only 48 years old. And within a few years he was famous throughout the world. Not for winning 20 games, which is all he ever really wanted, but because he had died of cancer, and the foremost cancer treatment center in the world was located in Seattle and named for Fred Hutchinson. I loved Hutch. I miss him.

Susan Tebbetts Mitchell on

Life with Birdie

I remember that as one of the few times Dad showed deep emotion. He was devastated when Fred died. Devastated. He looked like somebody had punched him in the stomach, for a long time. He really loved Fred. His buddy. I could tell, even as a kid, that Fred's death was a deep hurt when that happened.

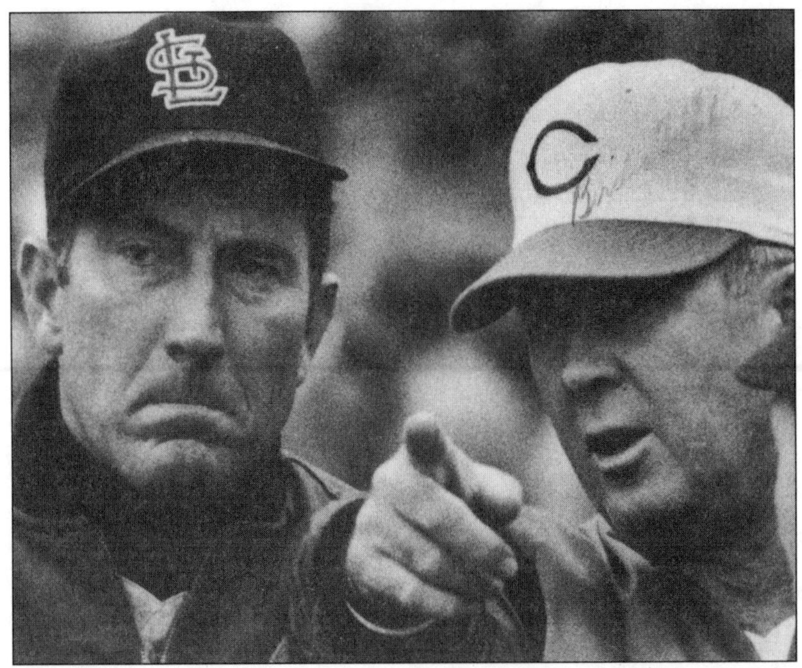

Me and Fred Hutchinson. We were golfing buddies, rival managers, and best friends. I was devastated when he died of cancer at only 48 years of age.

Whatever It Takes

I used to say I'd do anything to win as long as nobody got hurt. I've modified that principle over a long career. I don't believe in the corked bat. I don't believe in the spitball, though there was a time when I did. It's against the rules now, and I honor it in my old age. But in order to survive in the business it is imperative to compete at every legal level. And this is what I did without shame or mercy to Sam Mele, a dear friend of mine.

I don't remember who the umpires were–we could look it up–but Jim Kaat, who played for Minnesota, was pitching a game against me when I managed Cleveland. In about the second inning my coach, Tom Strickland, came over to me and said, "How about that shirt of Kaat's? It's hanging out of his jersey."

Patricia Tebbetts Kirton on

Life with Birdie

We lived in the penthouse at the Lakeshore Hotel overlooking Lake Erie. And when we got there, in the rooms there was fruit and wine and all kinds of goodies because Dad was the manager of the Cleveland Indians. And the first thing he did was to walk us around the whole hotel and introduce us to the person at the front desk, the person by the pool, the headwaiter, and he'd say, "These are my kids and they're going to be around and you'll see them, and if they give you any trouble I want to know." And then he would tell us, "I want you to treat everybody with a lot of respect, and don't be show-offs and don't be smart-mouths."

And then when we'd go to the Cleveland games. Mom would leave early to beat the traffic. Then we would get home and watch the rest of the game on TV and watch Dad on TV, and it was no big deal to us. That's just what Dad did. He was the manager of the Cleveland Indians. Down where you get your popcorn and hot dogs there's a room where all the baseball wives sit and wait for the players to come out of the clubhouse, and as kids we would get a little restless sitting in that room, so we would walk outside. There were all kinds of kids waiting for ballplayers' autographs. They'd say to us, "Who's your father?" We'd say, "Birdie Tebbetts." And they'd say, "Can we have your autograph?" "Sure!" And we'd start signing everything, and then, sure enough, Dad caught us doing that, and he blew his stack. He told us, "What have you ever done in your life to autograph anything for anybody?" He said, "You've done nothing. You've done nothing. Don't ever do that again!" But we thought it was pretty fun. Yeah, I remember the Lakeshore Hotel the best.

And I said, "Well, it's illegal as hell. But we'll let him go ahead and pitch with it until the time comes to issue a complaint, if that time ever comes. But there's no point in bringing it up here in the second inning." So the game went on, and it was one of those games, and Kaat has got us beat 1–0. We were having a helluva time getting men on base.

Sam Mele is my very, very dear friend from New England. We had barnstormed together in the old days, and he was now managing the Minnesota ballclub. In the ninth inning of the game we were at bat, two out, with a 1–2 count on our hitter, and I called time, walked up to the umpire, and said, "I want you to take a look at Kaat's jersey. It's frayed and it's below the shirt, and it's illegal as hell."

And the umpire said, "Birdie, the guy has been wearing the same shirt for nine goddamn innings. Do you mean to tell me that you're going to complain about it now?"

And I said, "I'm not only going to complain about it, but if you don't get him to change it right now, I'm going to play the game under protest, and you know damn well I can win it. And I'm not going to replay it from the ninth inning; I'm going to replay it from the beginning, because the shirt has been that way from the start."

Susan Tebbetts Mitchell on

Life with Birdie

After the games in Cleveland, he'd go back to the Lakeshore Hotel and put his feet up, and Mom would say to us, "Don't talk to your father. He's still back in the fifth inning." We'd have to wait and wait and wait. She'd finally ask him, "Are you almost done?" And he'd say, "Yeah." He was replaying the whole game in his head. Other times we'd be talking to him and Mom would say, "He's not listening. He's changing pitchers."

In a lot of ways he was very lucky that he married a woman like Mom, because she really was a great baseball wife. For a guy like Dad, she totally took care of everything else in his life. And even when he was there, she did not expect anything. She was the one who called him a friend of the family.

She loved being a baseball wife. She did. And she loved Dad. You could tell, she loved Dad. He was a unique guy.

Patricia Tebbetts Kirton on

Life with Birdie

One year during spring training in Tucson they were making a movie, and all the actors were staying at our hotel. Paul Newman was in it. *Hombre*, a Western, and we went out to the movie location. Cameron Mitchell invited us. And when we got back, Mom said, "Your father has had a heart attack." I was nine years old. But I remember that there was a priest and doctors and all these people around Dad in the bedroom. And one by one we came in and held his hand, and he said, "I love you and be good. Take care of your mother." Things like that. They took him to the hospital, and we would go visit him. Finally he got out of the hospital. He lived through the heart attack, which was great. He was a unique guy. And after a few months he went back to managing, but it couldn't last. And we checked out of the Lakeshore Hotel. For good.

Well, the umpire was about to say something when Mele came over. And Mele was trying to reason with his good friend Birdie.

"Birdie, the goddamn game is over! It's all over. Two men out in the ninth inning and you're up here. What the hell are you going to do?"

And I told him, "I'm going to have him change his shirt or you're going to lose the game, Sam."

And the umpire told Sam I was right. So they took Kaat, who was now mad, into the dugout. They corrected the shirt, and he came back out, his shirt no longer frayed. He stood there fuming on the mound. Then he walked the hitter on the next three pitches and threw a fat one up to Max Alvis, who hit it out of the ballpark. We beat Sam 2–1. And I ran like hell, because I knew Mele was going to kill me, and I didn't know how Kaat felt. But we won, and it created quite a stir, and they were quite upset. But as time went on it was one of the favorite stories Jim Kaat liked to tell on himself.

Marion, Virginia (Pop. 8,307)

In 1966, I had a heart attack. I really thought I was going to die. But I made a good recovery. George Strickland took over in the interim and in my absence the club went on a long winning streak. I sent George a telegram saying, "Dear George. Don't make it look so easy." I came back for a while, but it was too much. To try to manage in that highly charged competitive environment and raise a family was too much. I "resigned." I was 54 and out of work. That's how I ended up in Marion.

I looked around the main street of Marion, Virginia, and I had to laugh. Population: 8,307. Marion, Virginia, was a helluva

Family time in Marion. From left to right, that's Pat, Sue, me, Betty, George, and my wife, Mary. Photo courtesy John Dominis/TimePix.

long way from Cleveland, Ohio, where I had been manager of their baseball club a few months before. The Mets of Marion were in the Appalachian Rookie League, which was made up of teams from six towns that could be reached by bus in two hours or less. The players were kids–teenagers really–and they were green as hell. The ballpark was rustic, the lights were dim, and you had to walk up an embankment 150 yards to change and shower in the high school locker room. But as far as these kids were concerned they had arrived at the big time. It was unheard of for a guy who had managed a contending ballclub in the major leagues to take a job at the lowest possible rung of the baseball ladder. But at least I was still in baseball. And I was trying to prove to the world that I could still teach, and maybe with a little luck I would uncover some rookie talent for my new employers, the New York Mets. I was 55, had suffered a near-fatal heart attack the year before, had four kids and a wife who was a believer, and I loved baseball. A lot of guys said they wanted to stay in the game, but they didn't really mean it. I really meant it.

Susan Tebbetts Mitchell on

Life with Birdie

I suppose for Mom it was especially a big transformation. The next thing you know, being in that little cabin. But for us it was another adventure. That summer in Marion, Virginia, was a great summer. All the players and everybody at the ballpark were our age. These were young kids. We would go to these small, ramshackle, run-down ballparks. It was more like spring training. And I told Dad, "I think I like the catcher." His name was Tug. And he says, "No! No! Jesus Christ! Not him! He can't block. He can't throw! Hell, he can't even catch a ball!"

One of the difficulties of teaching a youngster is deciding which part of his game to concentrate on first. A kid may lack a good curveball and also need work on his move to first, so which do you pay attention to? I had to decide where to begin and what to leave to the next manager this kid would play for. At that level I had a lot of players to choose from. At one time I had 18 pitchers and 9 shortstops. This one kid, a pitcher, got on a winning streak and it went to his head. I had to cool him off when he tried to bring a rocking chair into the dugout.

Susan Tebbetts Mitchell on

Life with Birdie

Now, Dad traveled with the team, so Mom slept with a pistol under her pillow. And she locked her door when she went to bed and locked the front door when we went out. And when we would leave she'd say, "You better knock and tell me who you are." I was 15 at the time. Mom told us not to talk with anyone on the street because they were all hillbillies. Betty came back with a beard burn on her cheek, and she told Dad she had been down at the stables and this old man had grabbed her and tried to kiss her. And Dad flipped out! He said, "Jesus Christ! I'm going to go kill that guy!" And Mom said, "Don't, Birdie! Don't! You're going to have a heart attack. Don't leave. Call the cops. Please."

"I'm going to kill the son-of-a-bitch."

So Mom called the cops, and the cops told the guy to go over to the other side of the mountain and not to come back for the rest of the summer.

As kids we found that summer kind of exciting because all the ballplayers were more our age. In hindsight you realize the difference in the lifestyle, dramatic difference. After a lot of the games in Cleveland we all used to go to Cavoli's and sit in a big booth. There were pictures of us in that booth. And everybody would stop by, and it would be Birdie this and Birdie that. Then the next thing you know we were in this little cabin in hillbilly country, and Mom was sleeping with a gun, and you had to knock on the front door and say, "It's Sue. Don't shoot!" There it was. And we kids just had no idea of the loss Mom and Dad were suffering. After that summer we never went anywhere again. Birdie went by himself.

Patricia Tebbetts Kirton on

Life with Birdie

That was the trip for all of us. We went from the penthouse in Cleveland to Poplar Lodge in Marion, Virginia. That was the name of the house where we stayed. It was a two-bedroom, with a big living room and a kitchen, so Mom and Dad in one bedroom, all the girls in another, and George out in the living room on a pull-out couch. It was summer, and what we were going to do all summer was hang out at the Poplar Lodge. Dad taught us how to play solitaire. He got a big bowl of pennies, and we all played for money. That's a lot of what we did. We flipped the cards and won pennies, lost pennies, that kind of a thing. We played horseshoes in the backyard. And in the morning, you could hear these roosters. And when you'd be driving up this really rocky, unpaved, winding road, you'd look at people sitting on their porches and they had kind of blank stares on their faces. My Mom used to say, "They married their cousin, for God's sake!" These people just looked blank. And that was kind of funny. We also rode horses in Marion and went to the ballpark.

I tried to teach these young ballplayers something about baseball etiquette, and I vividly remember one day giving a seminar on autographing baseballs, telling them that the sweet spot between the close seams was reserved for stars or managers.

One evening we were all on the team bus coming back from a game and the guys were getting hungry, so I had the driver stop at a roadside restaurant outside of this Virginia town. As we strolled in, the restaurant owner said to me, "I can feed all you fellas, but your niggers will have to eat out in the back." I thought for a minute, and said, "How about take-out? Can you make up 150 sandwiches? I want to settle these guys into a motel." And the guy said, "Sure. The sandwiches will be ready in an hour." The team piled back onto the bus, and we drove out of that town and never looked back. I often wondered what that guy was going to do with 150 sandwiches.

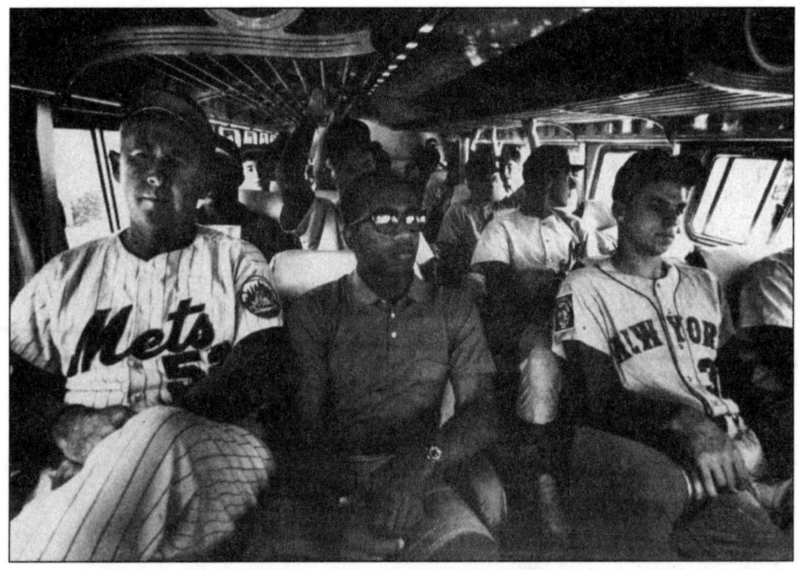

On the bus as manager of the Marion, Virginia, Mets—at the lowest possible rung of the baseball ladder after 11 years as a major league manager. Photo courtesy John Dominis/TimePix.

The Marion Mets turned out to be the last club I would ever manage. But that's OK. I was learning a new trade, learning to be a baseball scout, and finding out what it would take to be the best. It turned out being the best meant starting all over again at the very bottom.

Susan Tebbetts Mitchell on

Life with Birdie

We lived on a country road, a dirt road with all the mailboxes at the bottom of the road, and the first morning there I can remember the sound of this rooster. Cock-a-doodle-dooooo! Everybody jumped out of bed: "What is that? Oh my god!" After a while we began to like the rooster.

11

"Cave Ab Homine Unus Libri." *["Beware the man of one book."]*

–Thomas Aquinas

The Prophets

If you don't have a superior scouting staff and a superior development program you are not going to win. The only reason the Dodgers were better than anybody else except the Cardinals in the old days was that they had outstanding scouting and equally outstanding development. Branch Rickey ran both clubs. He's in the Hall of Fame. What else do you need to know about scouting?

You have to be a visionary. To be a scout you have to project. You have to take a raw baseball player, look at the unpolished talents he might posses, and project this into a vision of what he might become in the big leagues. And you have to have the background to make this assessment. The fact that his coach thinks he is great and his mother thinks he does well is not the determining factor.

When I was just starting out as a free-agent scout I used to be the last guy to go in to look at a player. One time I scouted a kid who made the big leagues and became a pretty good ballplayer. He was out of Atlanta, a Jewish kid. One of the difficulties of scouting free agents in high schools is that you are out there in the

Patricia Tebbetts Kirton on

Life with Birdie

Dad was a big influence on my daughter Jessica. She was going through a hard time when she was probably 14 or 15 or so, and Dad knew it. And when we would come over to the Island for a long visit, everyone would go to bed, but Jessica and Birdie would stay up and talk. And I would hear just bits and pieces of the conversation because I could hear them from the room where I was sleeping. He'd say, "Jessica, you need to think up here. Lofty thoughts. You need to think up here, not down here. Anybody who's down here, they're not good enough for you. You need to think up here." And I remember Jessica said, "I have a boyfriend." And Birdie said, "How are his grades?" Jessica said, "Good." And Dad said, "What sport does he play?" And Jessica said, "Soccer." And Birdie exclaimed, "Oh, no. Soccer is not a sport. Heck! Anybody can run!" And that really threw Jessica, because she was so proud that she was dating a person that was in a sport. So that was kind of funny. It's now a family joke about Birdie's estimate of soccer. "Hell! Anybody can run!"

countryside and wandering around these small towns, and you never know what diamond they're going to play on. And with this kid I had heard about, they changed the playing field several times because it had rained hard in the vicinity and all of the other diamonds had been washed out. I started real early in the morning after asking all over town. I finally found the place where these two high schools were to play.

The game started, although the weather was threatening, and the guy I came to see got up to hit. He hit a pop up. Foul fly. But it was a hell of a pop. There was something about his swing and the sound of his bat hitting the ball that reminded me of a great player I used to play against in the Texas League. And the next time up he hit an infield fly. Same thing. Same sound. And that's all he did. I put down in the report: "Outstanding major league prospect. Has tremendous power. Recommend highly."

And he was the No. 1 draft pick. But I only saw him

hit a fly ball two times at bat and then he got rained out. I never went back. The kid ended up as a DH for the Yankees. His name was Ron Blomberg, and he played about seven or eight years in the major leagues. That was back when I was at the bottom rung of scouting, scouting free agents a few years before moving up as senior scout of the Yankees.

In 28 years of scouting for the Mets, the Yankees, the Orioles, and finally the Marlins I learned a few golden rules. As a matter of fact I wrote a pamphlet about scouting, and somebody found it and published it. But what the hell, it wasn't the first time I'd been plagiarized. Here's what I call the Golden Rules of scouting:

Golden Rules

1. Remember who told you.
2. Be open to a change of mind. Ballplayers can improve or decline suddenly and remarkably.
3. Your evaluation of a player must be a tightly held secret and is solely owned by your employer.
4. Finally, seldom confirm, never deny, always distinguish.

Let me explain that last one. Seldom confirm: don't ever say a guy can absolutely do something because ballplayers are frail human beings and there are times when the gods are unsmiling. Never deny: just because you've never seen the guy do it does not mean that the guy will never be able to do it. Always distinguish: make the distinction between what you have seen and what you have heard.

Chores of the Master Scout

A master scout's chores do not end with making appraisals of multimillion-dollar talents. I'll give you an example. Gabe Paul called me in and said, "We can't sign Mickey Rivers. We can't even find him. Find out where he is and go sign him." And I said, "How much?" and he told me. I had an idea where to look for him.

Years before I had scouted Mickey Rivers as a high school prospect and drafted him and found out that I couldn't sign him because he was on probation for stealing a car. Ha. Anyway, I found him in downtown Cleveland with a girl, and the story of signing him with the girl around is really cute. After asking around a bit, I went to a club the lowlife of Cleveland went to all the time. It's famous; it's a half-assed whorehouse, hotel, bar, and grill. And there in a booth across the room was Mickey with a girl. I told the owner, "Have somebody tell me who the girl is that is with that guy." And I said, "Treat the kid as if he was a king and put everything on the house." And the owner, who was in the Mafia, said OK.

So Mickey saw me and came by with the girl and I said, "Hi, how are you, Mickey. I understand you two are good friends. I want you to have a wonderful time." He left and went back to his booth. They had dinner and then Mickey and his girl went off somewhere to be private. I was sitting at my table and a guy came and sat down with me and said, "That's Jimmy Brown's mistress that kid is with. They're not going together now. She's a whore. A $50 whore." And I said, "Thank you. That's all I want to know."

Patricia Tebbetts Kirton on

Life with Birdie

Because he was gone so much when we were growing up he wasn't involved in our school; he wasn't involved with our extracurricular activities or our friends. But he appreciated them. I was doing some ballet at the time, and he would be the first one to get out there and describe it into his tape recorder. "Now Patricia will be doing a ballet dance." He carried that recorder with him all the time, and he'd say, "And she looks lovely today." And I'd do my ballet dance and he'd be recording everything. "Now she's making a beautiful pirouette." Just a character. And I'd say, "Da-a-a-d."

The next day I went back to the club and there was Mickey with the girl. By now I was negotiating the contract with him. But every time I said something and made an offer, he looked at her and she went, "Uh-uh. I don't think so." I knew that they were half bagged. No matter what I offered, she had the veto.

After a while Mickey went to the bathroom. While he was gone I said to her, "I'll give you $1,000 cash, or a mink coat worth more than $1,000, if you sign on the next offer."

"You will?" she asked.

I said, "Yes." So Mickey came back and sat down, ordered another drink, and we beat around and beat around and I said, "Well, I'm going to make you just one more offer, Mickey, and it's more than I'm allowed to make. Here it is." And I laid it out, and he looked and put his head down and he looked over at her. After a few seconds she nodded and said, "Yeah, I think so." And he said OK.

So I called Gabe and I said, "This is what I offered Mickey Rivers. This is what he has accepted and if there are any other fringe benefits, I'll take care of those myself." And he said, "OK, put him on." So Rivers got on the phone. I walked by the girl and whispered, "What's your name?" And she told me. So I went in the other room and wrote out a check for $1,000. I came in and gave it to her and she looked at it and it disappeared somewhere. And so Mickey Rivers signed with the New York Yankees. But the end of the story is that when my check to that girl came back, it had seven names written on the back of it.

It's funny how some names keep moving in and out of your life. You take Luis Tiant. Cuban pitcher. Right-hander. He was that roly-poly guy with the Fu Manchu mustache throwing for the Red Sox against the Yanks in that crazy playoff race in 1978. Anyway, Al Rosen was new with the Yankees front office, and after that season with the Red Sox Luis Tiant was a free agent, so Al sent me up to Boston to sign him.

Betty Tebbetts Deluca on

The Rochester Episode

He was in the airport in St. Louis about to get on a plane to Rochester and he thought he might be having heart attack, but he needed to get to Rochester. So he wrote a note that said something to the effect of, "I am having a heart attack. My name is. . . . My wife's name is. . . . These are the medications I take. If you find me dead, I had a heart attack." And he got on the plane.

When the plane took off, he folded this note up, gave it to the flight attendant, and said, "Don't open this note until the plane lands." Then he took out his tape recorder and started recording, "I am having a heart attack." This is the part we heard, and I don't remember all of it, but he said, "The pain is great. I've taken a Valium. I've taken a nitro." And then he started going through and saying, "George, Pat, Betty, Sue, Mary, I love you and don't feel bad about me. I've had a good life." So he had the presence of mind to do that.

And then you could hear the flight attendant saying, "We have your note. We're going to land you in Indianapolis. We have an ambulance crew and will take you off." And Dad was refusing to go. "I'm not getting off the plane. You can land in Indianapolis, but I'm not getting off the plane."

He then documented a little bit more about his life and what he had done, giving a little history, reliving his life as he thought it was about to end.

You could hear one of the pilots saying, "We're landing the plane in Indianapolis." Dad once again: "I'm not getting off. You can land it if you want, but I refuse to get off the plane." So they chose not to land, and in Rochester there was an ambulance waiting, but Dad still refused to get off. He had these huge metal cases with his scouting reports locked inside. You could stand on them, that's how hard they were. But he felt if anybody got ahold of that, they could undermine–I don't know what he thought. But he was not going to let go of them. And you know his hands are huge and strong, so he had them in his fists and he refused to get off the plane or let go. He refused to let go of them until the manager of this Triple A team in Rochester, Greg Biagini was found. Mom and I flew to Rochester to be with him.

Greg Biagini
(Manager of the Yankees' Rochester Farm Club) on

The Rochester Episode

We were going to be in the playoffs against Columbus and Birdie was supposed to scout them and bring us a report. Well, we were in our clubhouse at the ballpark waiting. His plane had arrived and he hadn't checked into his hotel. Where the hell was he? And then we got a call from the hospital saying they had this guy in intensive care who was driving them crazy because he wanted to talk with us. So three of us went over, and there was Birdie in bed, all hooked up with wires and blinking lights with tubes in him. He said, "Take this down." And the three of us grabbed pen and paper and he started to talk. He was giving us a page-by-page scouting report on each Columbus player. From memory! And as I'm writing as fast as I can, I look for a second into this guy's eyes. They are blue. They are bright blue eyes and they are having a ball! This guy is about to die and he's showing off how goddamn smart he is. I'll never forget the look on his face as long as I live. I ran into him a year later. Still going. Like that rabbit on TV.

This will show you how things have changed in 40 years. Even though Tiant had that jerky motion bringing the ball down before the throw, Ballanfant wouldn't call it a balk because he said there was no attempt to deceive. Well, anyway, I always liked Luis, and he liked me. He had a keen sense of humor, a giggle. He laughed like a lady. Gabe Paul and I signed him for the Reds years before when we took a tour of Cuba back before the Bay of Pigs fiasco made travel to Cuba prohibited. And after we'd signed Luis and we had a couple of other players to use as trade bait, Gabe and I left for the winter minor league meeting in Nashville and the major league meeting three days later in San Francisco. We were so broke in those days that Gabe intended to sell one of the players for $15,000 to pay our travel expenses. Luis Tiant was one of the players we tried to peddle. My dear friend Fred Hutchinson was

> **Patricia Tebbetts Kirton on**
>
> **Life with Birdie**
>
> Betty had bought a beautiful new home in New Hampshire, and she had decorated it really lovely. She and her two kids were excited that Dad was on the road nearby and was going to stop by to see her. So he knocked on the door and she was all excited and she opened the door and as he walks into her beautiful new home she asked, "Dad, how do you like it?" And he said, "Black." Betty said, "What? What? What do you mean?" He said, "I like my coffee black." Because he doesn't think about homes and nice furniture and doesn't think to say, "What a beautiful home, Betty. You've done well, Betty." Just "I like my coffee black." Dad would not notice things like how a house was decorated. That was not part of his vocabulary.

managing the Cards at the time, and when I tried to deal him to Fred he just laughed. But Luis later won 10 games for me his first year up in Cleveland in 1964. But now I was senior scout for the Yankees, and when Luis became available at a time when the Yanks needed an extra right-hander I called him up and set up a meeting for dinner at a hotel in Boston. The Ritz. I got there early, handed the headwaiter $20, and told him that I wanted a remote table and that after my guests were seated we were not to be disturbed till I gave the signal. So Luis and his wife came in, and we sat down and chatted about old times.

Now here's what I mean by certain names coming in and out of your life. Luis' father had been given special permission by Fidel Castro to come to Boston to watch Luis pitch in the World Series. The press made a big deal of it–the proud old man sitting in the stands to watch Luis pitch in the big time. Well, how's this for things coming around and around? Almost 40 years before, right after the 1940 Series, which I played in, Charlie Gehringer and I took our Series money and went on a cruise to Cuba. Charlie's off-season job was as a manufacturer's rep in the auto business, and when we got to Havana his company connections saw to it that we were driven everywhere by a chauffeured limo. We ended up one day in box seats at the Havana ballpark, and between innings we were introduced over the loudspeaker as two American players who had just played in the Detroit World Series. We stood up and everybody cheered and yelled, and it kept up so we stood again. But the real story is that the pitcher for Havana in that game was a man named Tiant whose wife had just given birth to a son named Luis.

So here was that same baby Luis in front of me, and I've got to sign him for the Yankees. We talked it through, made a deal, airtight, no other questions. We shook on it, and Luis was to come to New York the next day and sign, so I signaled the waiter, and we ordered, ate, and said see you tomorrow. I called Al Rosen and told him we'd made a deal and would be in the next day for the signing. Great.

The next day we were sitting in the Yankees office. Al Rosen was there. I was there, Luis Tiant and Mrs. Tiant were there, and Luis has his pen poised over the contract. Everyone was holding his breath when Luis said, "I want a bonus to sign." And Al Rosen looked at me and said, "I thought you said this deal was set." So I said to Luis, "Luis, if you do well for the Yanks this year you will get a bonus." And Luis said, "I want $25,000 to sign this contract." Al looked at me again, and I shrugged. We went back and forth, and finally I said, "How about this, Luis? You sign, and if you do well for the Yanks you'll get a $25,000 bonus at the end of the season." And Luis said, "Who says whether I do well for the Yanks?" And I pointed to myself, and I said, "I'll make that call, Luis. OK?" He said "OK" and he signed. He went on to win 13 games that year after Tommy John and Ron Guidry.

The evening after my meeting with the Tiants in Boston I drove the 40 miles up to Nashua and stopped in to see Sis and then over to call on Betty and her kids. I had forgotten about that promise of a bonus to Tiant, and it was getting late into September when I passed George Steinbrenner in the hall one day. He looked at me and I said, "Did you ever pay that kid his $25,000?" He laughed. And the bonus was quickly taken care of.

As with Luis Tiant I came to appreciate the skills of Latin players early on. He played for me at Cleveland. Other clubs ignored them in those early days, except the Dodgers. I like the Latinos, the Puerto Ricans, Dominicans, Cubans, and so forth, because baseball is their life. They live the game and love it. And the players are all family oriented. They have such loyalty.

Emotions play such an important part in the judgment calls we make. I sometimes wonder how a rich person comes to decide that a painting is worth a $1 million or $2 million or whatever. There was this time when New York was ready to sign free agents and this one particular kid's name came up. He was a 14th-place draft choice, but he was also the son of an old Yankees ballplayer and George Steinbrenner said to sign him as a first-pick draft choice. And the chief scout of the New York Yankees stood up and said signing the kid was a mistake for a lot of reasons having nothing to do with baseball. As the argument got more heated the scout had had enough. He stood up, looked George straight in the eye, and said, "George, you sign that kid and I quit." And by golly George backed down.

I got back to my hotel one day and there was a message from the Yankees general manager, and when he came on the line he said, "I want you to go out and sign Billy Martin to manage the Yankees. Then I want you to bring him to New York right away. Nobody must hear about this. Don't let word of this leak out under any circumstances. Fly him to New York under an assumed name and bring him directly to the ballpark. (At this time, in 1975 Yankee Stadium was under repair and Yankees games were being played in the Mets' Shea Stadium.) I said, "OK. Where is he?" And he said, "I don't know. Nobody knows. Find him." I said

The Levels of

Scouting

Bird Dog: A scout that covers a local area of high schools and colleges, usually does not get paid, and usually scouts for the experience or to be affiliated with a major league team; sometimes paid a commission on a premium draft choice; scouts guys that are eligible for the June draft and is usually hand-picked by the area scout; is usually a high school or college coach.

Part-Time Scout: The same as a bird dog in his duties but usually gets compensated with a small salary.

Free-Agent Scout: A scout that covers high schools and colleges for the June draft; in the summer covers the minor leagues for trades; some have a major league team to cover but it depends on how their club operates. Some clubs have these guys cover all levels of a team from short-season A to the major leagues.

Crosschecker or Supervisor: Has a designated area to cover and checks out the top prospects in that area; also covers minor league teams in the summer; better known as pro coverage. Usually teams have three crosscheckers: one for the east, one for the midwest, and one for the west.

National Crosschecker: Travels across the country giving a third opinion on the top draft choices recommended by the crosschecker and free-agent scouts; also has pro coverage and usually covers the major league teams.

Scouting Director: Oversees the operation of all of the above and spends a lot of time on the road seeing the top draft choices like the national crosschecker.

Pro Scout: Covers major league teams and sometimes minor league teams; usually works closely with the general manager and recommends players for possible trades.

Advance Scout: Goes in advance of the team gathering offensive and defensive information on how to play the opposing team.

"OK" and hung up. Then I got out my black book and started thumbing through it for the names and numbers of guys who were Martin's drinking buddies.

Now Billy Martin had been a colorful second baseman for the Yankees in the fifties, and after kicking around the league he ended up managing in Minnesota, Detroit, and Texas. He was tempestuous–hard drinking and stormy–and was given to tantrums around home plate. I'd heard stories of his upbringing in the back alleys of Oakland and was not surprised at the fire in his temperament.

After about eight phone calls I flew to Denver, rented a car, and drove into the mountains to a mining town called Central City. I parked my car and started walking down main street looking into every bar. I finally found Billy in back of a smoky saloon. His marriage was breaking up and he was out of a job, and the salary offer of $75,000 looked pretty good, so he signed and we headed for Denver. I bought him a one-way ticket to New York under the name of John Smith or something and off we went.

Now my instructions were to deliver him to the ballpark without attracting the attention of the press. More easily said than done. We got into New York late and checked into the Park Central, and no sooner had Billy closed his door than he called an old drinking buddy and arranged a rendezvous. I found Mickey Mantle and Billy Martin in a nearby pub. Being a compulsive collector, before breaking it up I took a paper napkin, handed it to Mickey, and said, "Sign this, Mickey." He did, and I looked at it and it said, "Fuck you Birdie, Mickey Mantle." Then I delivered Martin's live body to the clubhouse of Shea Stadium to an eagerly awaiting George Steinbrenner. As it was, Billy arrived on Old-Timers' Day, and in the ceremony introducing all the immortals, including DiMaggio and Mantle and the descendants of Ruth and Gehrig, the last to be introduced was to be the

Susan Tebbetts Mitchell on

Life with Birdie

I left Florida when I was 19 to go to California to join Pat. She went when she was 17. Living in Anna Maria Island was like not living in the United States. It was remote and small, and Pat and I always wanted to get out. So at 19 I went to California. Pat had called me and said, "I'm in a town in California. Mammoth Lake, California. A ski resort. And there isn't an old person in the town."

I said, "You're kidding me."

"Nope. Behind every cash register is a young person."

I said, "OK, I'm flying out."

I said "good-bye" and Mom was standing in the driveway kind of crying. And Betty was standing alongside her saying, "Sue, I don't know why you're doing this to Mom. You'll be back. You know you'll be back."

So I left.

And after that the only time we really saw Dad was when he would come out at least twice a year wherever we were. He would find a ballplayer he could scout close to us. So when we were in that ski area by Tahoe, he found a ballplayer in Sacramento. He would call and say, "The closest I can get is Sacramento, baby."

And after that it stopped snowing and we both moved to L.A. And then it was easy time, even though Pat and I lived close to the poverty line for a long while. A nice apartment in Studio City. But Dad would call and say, "I'm coming to a game."

When he was scouting for the Yankees, he would fly in ahead of them to scope out the Angels before the Yankees would play them. Wow! Pat and I would head for his hotel, get in our bathrobes, order room service, and say, "Hello, good-bye, Dad."

He'd say, "Get what you want. Have a good time. I'll be back." He'd go to the game, and we'd order up. We really had a blast. We felt like we had money. We would go down after the game, and Birdie would arrive and everybody would fuss. We'd have a drink and he'd have coffee, and all the players would be moving around, and for a few days he would transform our lives again. And then before he left he'd say, "You need anything?"

"Nope." Then he'd fly out and we'd go back to our normal existence.

> **Patricia Tebbetts Kirton on**
>
> **Life with Birdie**
>
> A reporter from the *Islander* newspaper, asked Birdie, "What do you want to be known as? When you pass away, how do you want to be remembered? What are you proud of?" And Dad said, "I'm just a baseball guy. It's all I've ever been. It's all I ever wanted to be." And Sue whispered to me–and Sue laughed at this–"Funny he wouldn't say, 'As a great father, as a great husband, as a great provider.'" He was all of those things, but he never thought of himself in those terms. He did them, but he didn't think of them. "Just a ballplayer, just a ball guy, a baseball guy."

new manager of the New York Yankees, Billy Martin. The crowd went wild.

A major league scout who is in fact a major league scout and who only scouts at the major league level has a tremendous amount of responsibility. It's an entirely different type of scouting. It all depends on the guy and how much authority he has and whether he can walk into the general manager's office, sit down, and make sense and save everybody a lot of time.

When you talk about scouts you are talking about me when I started. I was scouting free-agent players. First it was kids in high school or college and then I moved into professionals. In five or six years I was an accepted, accredited free-agent scout. And that's why I'm listed in that scouting directory. You can look through that and you won't recognize hardly any of the names. Yet there are some powerful men in that book. Take for instance Tony Lucadello. Tony was an infielder with the St. Louis Browns. Then there's Joe Branzell, who was one of the most famous East Coast scouts because he would write a book on scouting every year. He scouted out of Baltimore. He played very, very little ball, but he was an exceptional scout. Still, he had no power inside the office. Just scouting power. And there was George Genovese, one of the greatest scouts that ever lived. He signed some of the greatest ballplayers of all time. He signed Frankie Robinson. He signed Vada Pinson. He signed out on the West Coast. He did not play much, if any, pro ball, but his brother, Chick Genovese, did. Another great scout, Tom Ferrick, was also a great pitching coach.

The money a player is worth is not important to the scout. The general manager wants to know who is available and what they want. If a guy is the kind of a scout that I have in mind, the general manager of the club that he is talking to knows that the scout will convey the facts to the general manager with an opinion attached. The other kind of scout, a free-agent scout, starts at the major league level, either for experience or because he lives close to a ballclub, and they say, "Go in and take a look at Atlanta for their next homestand." So that's what he does. He doesn't know why, what, where, or how, but that's what they told him to do. Major league scouts get called in and they say, "We have a deal involving So-and-So. Go take a look at him and give us a report on whether he would fit in with our ballclub." One guy scouts the talent and the other guy scouts the need of this team.

Mark Lemke is the second baseman of the Atlanta ballclub. He doesn't run and he doesn't have any power. Those are all the things he doesn't do. But the things that he does do, and does well, fit the Atlanta ballclub so well that he actually is a star without the talent of a star.

I call guys like that "Joes." The Joes are the guys who win you the pennant. They are the guys that, all of a sudden, you look up and they are going to pinch hit with a man on third and one man out. And when the pitch is thrown to him you know damn well he's going to hit a fly ball. Or there's a guy on first base, and you know when you put on a hit-and-run, he's going to make contact. With a guy on second and nobody out, you know that even though he makes an out he's going to hit a groundball to the right side of the diamond. Those are the things that win ballgames.

When you're signing a guy you've got to decide not only would he help us but also has he the talents we need and is he available. You recommend on that basis. Oftentimes that's where things get off-kilter. A deal is made without the understanding of the limitations of the recommendation and evaluation of the trade. Everybody looks up and asks, "What the hell are they going to want of this guy? Why sign this guy and give up a pitcher to get him?" And the answer is that they need him and they have a pitcher to spare. The pitcher they give up is going to be a good one, *but* the guy they get is like that little second baseman Lemke.

Joes are just guys who think of it as a job. Most of them seem to have a certain attitude. I think they understand what they can do and what they are required to do, and they're willing to do it *if they are appreciated.* You've got to let that guy know what you need and that you don't expect him to do everything. And then you got a guy who understands what his role is. So a guy comes along and you say he's a role ballplayer, he's a Joe, he fits the need of a club. And this Joe is very valuable. For instance, say you need a second-string catcher and you've got a guy who is hitting for you who is a helluva catcher. All of a sudden your catcher gets on in the ninth inning and if you can get a helluva defensive catcher who can run a little faster, he could take the place of the guy, run for him, and go back, and you wouldn't even feel anything. You'd have that little bit of an edge that you needed in the ninth inning. For a Joe to be effective the manager must understand what he is and what he can do. Then when the bell rings the manager will put him in a situation that he deserves to be in. But if you don't use him properly you don't have very much. If you don't have a superior scouting staff and a superior development program you are not going to win.

The Remarkable Bucky Dent

The Yankees had a young left-handed pitcher, a rookie named Guidry, and Chicago wanted and needed a left-hander. Now before describing this deal let me recite a bromide you hear a lot in the front office: some of the best trades are the ones that are never made. This is one of those. Chicago wanted Guidry, an untried rookie, and the Yankees needed a shortstop, which Chicago had. This shortstop is a Joe. He doesn't have much range, can't steal a base, takes short leads. These are all the things he can't do. But he always turns the routine plays. He hits behind the runner. He lays down the bunt and it goes fair. He makes contact on a hit-and-run. His name is Dent. Bucky Dent. The Yankees kept Guidry, acquired Bucky Dent, and a year later Guidry won 25 games and Dent hit a home run against the Red Sox in the winner-take-all tiebreaker to win the pennant, then hit .417 in a barrage of singles, helping the Yanks win the World Series in six.

Ron Guidry was a brilliant pitcher. A left-hander. He won 25 games his second year up, the same year Billy Martin got fired for making some remarks about George Steinbrenner. Bob Lemon took over in midseason and led the team to a World Series win over the Dodgers–the same Series in which a Joe named Bucky Dent was dazzling at shortstop and in the clutch. Anyway, the season was over and the contracts had gone out to the players, and most of them had been signed and returned. All except Ron Guidry's.

He was a splendid fellow. Guidry knew exactly who he was and where he came from, which happened to be somewhere deep in the swamps of Louisiana. He was a Cajun. Old family. When Guidry's contract didn't come back Gabe Paul said, "Birdie, you better go down there and see what's going on." So I flew to New Orleans, got a car, and drove a few hours along the banks of bayous, stopping once in a while to ask the way, until I finally got to this sleepy little town where Guidry was supposed to live. Well, it seemed as though there were 10,000 Guidrys in this Louisiana parish. Finally somebody said I might find the guy I was looking for down this road and to look for a house that was being built. I pulled up to a stop by this half-framed house, got out of the car, and started walking toward it when a voice yelled out, "Hey, Birdie! What the hell are you doing here?" I looked up and way up there on top of the frame of the roof, hanging by his fingertips, was a million-dollar 25-game winner with a hammer in his left hand and a grin on his face a mile wide. I wanted to tell him to get the hell down from those rafters before he broke his goddamn neck and plunged the Yankees organization into the cellar, but I was afraid to distract him.

He had yelled, "What the hell are you doing here?" But we both knew the answer. I watched anxiously as he hopped from beam to rafter, finally hitting the ground. We shook hands and retreated to the kitchen of his old house. We had some coffee and a bowl of Mrs. Guidry's gumbo while these little kids scooted around between our legs. Mrs. Guidry was an awfully nice woman, and we began talking about what it was like being a housewife from the bayou living in the New York vicinity with kids to raise and a husband on the road much of the time. She just happened to mention that she often felt out of place in those malls outside New York among all those stylish people wearing those clothes with the little alligators on them. I knew the brand because Mary had a few of the outfits. I knew they came in all sizes and colors for men, women, and children. And I could tell from just having driven through it that you could bet your sweet ass these fancy alligator clothes were not for sale in the Guidrys' hometown.

So I said to Mrs. Guidry, "You and your family would look great in those outfits. And so would Ron. When you step off the

plane in New York you should be wearing them. And so should Ron. And your children! Complete outfits. And you will. By express mail. Before the week is out." She smiled broadly and I pulled out the contract and asked Ron to sign.

As I was driving out of Ron Guidry's hometown, with a signed contract in my pocket, I had to stop at the local drugstore and pick up a packet of Tums. It helped, but that gumbo stayed with me all the way home.

Winfield

One summer I spent a long, long time in San Diego, a National League city, because at the end of that season Dave Winfield would become a free agent, and the Yankees organization was interested in him. And this is where a senior scout earns his pay. Millions of dollars are riding on his recommendation.

The championship ring I received for the Yankees' 1977 World Series victory (top), and the one I got for the Florida Marlins' 1997 World Series victory.

Susan Tebbetts Mitchell on

Life with Birdie

After he left the Yankees he went with the Baltimore Orioles and worked out of Chicago so he could scout both leagues without traveling. He and Mom lived at the River Plaza. It was right on the river, an apartment high-rise with a restaurant on the ground floor. He transformed that apartment–scouting papers all over the place. When he went to the ballpark he'd go down the elevator to the curb to catch a cab. That was when he could hardly walk. I could not believe he could make it into the ballpark. He'd make the cab stop at a special place. He couldn't climb steps. He was close to 80 at that point. That was the last summer he worked. He loved that moment. That's the kind of life he liked: room service, maids, restaurants. He had it all there.

The questions are many. First, is the prospect in good physical condition? To find out you have to go to the ballpark, take a seat in the stands, and watch the whole ballgame, including the pregame practice. Does he run sprints? How does he handle himself among the other players? What does he look like in batting practice? When the game begins, does he hustle? Does he run out a pop fly to the infield? What does his swing look like? How does he respond to a called third strike?

This is an excerpt from a 12-page report I wrote on Dave Winfield:

> The poor hitch and the strength of Jimmie Foxx; it's easy to criticize the former and admire the latter. Great velocity in arm. He has flaws like all big swingers. He can be had but if he is to be great he will adjust. And if not he will be all star. Makes big parks look small. Slow getting started. Legs too long. Accelerates for long run. Not quick.

Jimmie Foxx was a great hitter, and when he swung he had a little hitch. Same thing with Dave Winfield. That's what Gary Sheffield does, too. The first thing you say to yourself when you see him swing is, " You can't do that." And then you say to yourself "Well, Foxx did it." A hitch is a bad thing. But Foxx did it. And so did Winfield and so did Mel Ott. Anyway, when you are going to spend a million dollars to obtain a ballplayer you have to understand that, no matter how great the talent, he is a human being and he might have all the frailties that the rest of humanity is subject to. Where does he go when the ballgame is over? Is he a boozer? Women? And nowadays the question of drugs is always of concern. To find out what is going on, a $20 tip to a hotel bellhop can save a ballclub millions.

The Yankees signed Dave Winfield for $1.5 million. He played for the Yankees for eight years, and one year he missed the batting crown by a mere three points.

But not every deal works out as hoped. With the Yankees no deal was concluded without the approval of George himself. In one instance a deal was made, and it was a deal for a ballplayer that I did not endorse. It turned out to be a bad deal, both for the Yankees and for the player. It may have been just a passing remark that George made to a reporter in an elevator, but I heard about the remark when I landed in Tampa on my way home from a trip. I read the squib in the paper, something about the deal and George's comment that, "these things happen. You know, Birdie is getting on in years." As soon as I read that I turned on my heels and I bought a ticket then and there back to New York. When I got to New York I headed straight for George's office. Somebody yelled, "Hey, you can't go in there!" And I said, "Try to stop me." And I walked in without knocking.

I said, "George, I can't work for you anymore."

And he said, "OK. I understand." And I went home.

Betty Tebbetts Deluca on

Life with Birdie

Dad, of course, was sick. He was 80 years old. People who knew him knew he was sick. But he didn't act sick. And he didn't always look sick. But he had a bad, bad heart, and he did have a handicap sticker in his car. And one time when he pulled up into this handicapped parking space and got out, this older lady went running after him, screaming, "You are abusing the handicapped sticker system. There's nothing wrong with you! Look at you! You're fine! What's wrong with you that you deserve a handicapped sticker?" And Dad just looked at her and smiled and said, "I have a cold," and kept on walking.

The Hall of Fame

As I look back I can see that I have been very, very fortunate. I have played major league baseball for 16 years. I've been chosen for three All-Star teams. I have played in a World Series. I have caught the greatest pitchers of my time. I have managed three major league clubs. I have been honored by the national media and have been generously praised in the autobiographies of the great players against whom I once competed. I have been a front office guy, an executive vice president, and I then quit to manage a ball club. Finally, I have been a senior scout for winning clubs for the last 28 years of my life. Not many ballplayers have had that many jobs in baseball over their careers.

Entry into the Baseball Hall of Fame has eluded me, but that's OK with me. There is no category in the Hall of Fame for the kind of career I've had in baseball. But the Hall of Fame has touched my life in a direct way because I was honored to serve for a number of years on the Hall's Veterans Committee. Because the Veterans Committee is one of only two gateways for entry, in that capacity I have learned how selections are made.

I would like to pause here and talk about a couple of reporters. One day they were sharing a ride to Candlestick Park out near the airport in San Francisco. They were almost out of gas, so they stopped at a filling station and pulled up to the pump and waited while this fat old guy came walking out with splay feet, wearing greasy overalls. The driver said, "Fill it up," and the old guy went about his business. One of the reporters looked at him, and looked again, and thought he saw something familiar in the way this guy walked and also in the size of his nose. And so he got out of the car and went up to the guy and said, "Aren't you Ernie Lombardi?"

And the guy who was pumping the gas said, "Yes, I am."

And the reporter said. " I remember you. Cincinnati Reds, right?"

And Ernie Lombardi said, " That's right. That was a long time ago. But I'm doing OK now." And the reporter paid for the gas and shook Ernie's hand, got in the car, and they drove off.

Now Ernie Lombardi was a catcher when I was a catcher, a little older by about five years, and unlike me he played in the National League. Lombardi could hit like hell. He hit over .300 10 times. He won the batting title twice. He was voted Most Valuable Player in 1938 and played in eight All-Star games. He played in two World Series, and in one of those Series he played against me. And he ended up pumping gas at a filling station in San Francisco.

But Ernie Lombardi is not remembered for pumping gas or for being Most Valuable Player. He is remembered best for what the writers gleefully called "the Snooze." That play was not his fault, nor did it have anything to do with the outcome of the game or the loss of the 1939 World Series against the New York Yankees. This is why I chose to speak up in the first meeting I attended as a member of the Veterans Committee of the Hall of Fame. It could even be the very reason why I was chosen to sit on the Veterans Committee.

This so called "snooze" play that froze in the public mind is also the least important thing about this guy Lombardi's career.

Here's what happened. The Yankees had taken the first three games in the 1939 World Series against Cincinnati. It was 0–0 going into the seventh inning when the Yankees went ahead 2–0. By the ninth the Reds were ahead 4–2 and the Yankees tied it, so it went into extra innings. Frank Crosetti walked, moved to second on a sacrifice, and got to third when Charlie Keller got to first on an error. So you've got Keller on first, Crosetti on third, no outs, and up came DiMaggio, who hit a shot to right scoring Crosetti. That broke the tie, but the outfielder bobbled the ball and Keller, a big, burly guy, headed for home. He smashed into Ernie Lombardi, knocking him senseless, with the ball lying a few feet away. DiMaggio saw this and streaked home; he scored with Ernie still lying there in the dust.

As far as the press was concerned, the story of that Series was not that it was a four-game sweep. The press made the story of the Series the fact that Lombardi lay senseless at home plate while DiMaggio scored. And that story was a nonstory because before Lombardi got knocked out, the winning run had already scored. Keller and DiMaggio's runs were not needed. But the press had a field day with Lombardi's misfortune.

That story had fixed itself in the mind of this one reporter who was serving with me on the Veterans Committee of the Hall of Fame. I believed Lombardi was being treated unfairly, and I was going to do something about it. No matter that Ernie died before I was put on the committee. It was a very, very personal grudge that kept him out. Ernie would get within three votes of getting elected and these guys would block it. So at my first meeting I said, "I'd like to talk about Lombardi." And one of my friends, Bob Broeg, who was a famous writer and had written novels and thousands of baseball articles, said, "Birdie, we have discussed him at length." And I said, "Not on my watch you haven't. This is my first meeting." I said, "You don't have a Hall of Fame without Ernie Lombardi in it. It's not fair."

Now the three guys who wouldn't vote for him were listening. They were voting Ernie out of the Hall of Fame for a personal reason. He got knocked out at home plate and he had attempted to commit suicide and yes, he went a little bad mentally later on in life. But he bounced back and died peacefully. I said, "It's a great honor for me to be on this committee, and I know the people who are responsible for me being here and I'm thanking you now for putting me on, but I know you put me on because you knew I was going to pop off. And I'm popping off right now."

After it was over, Gabe Paul and I had coffee. Gabe and I always had coffee before and after the meetings. I said, "How did you vote?" And he said, " Out of respect for you I did not vote. I could not vote for that man." I said, "You did not vote for him because of your dislike of him in your days as the Reds' traveling secretary. It has nothing to do with his ability as a baseball player."

It took a while. Some members of the committee had to retire before it happened. In any case, when you walk through the Hall of Fame in Cooperstown today, you might pause by the bronze plaque to Ernie Lombardi. In some funny way having Ernie hanging up there makes me feel that even I made it into those hallowed halls.

Scouts and the Hall of Fame

There are no scouts in the Hall of Fame. Over the years there have been initiatives to have the scouts recognized in the Hall. Each year the proposal is voted on by the committee and gets sent to the board of directors and each year it never gets by. They will not admit that they have eliminated anybody from eligibility. I've heard it said that they say, "The scouts are probably right, but why should we change? We're not getting pressure from outside except an occasional article." At one point they came to me and said, "Birdie, we'll open up a section in the Hall of Fame to honor all scouts."

Not good enough. Not at all. Because the Hall of Fame is intended to honor individual achievement.

Back with Roland Hemond

Roland Hemond had become general manager of the Baltimore club, and he set it up so that Mary and I could live in Chicago for the summer. That way I could scout both leagues for the Orioles. It was one of the happiest times of our lives. We loved living in Chicago. Our daughter Sue and her family lived nearby, so we saw a lot of them. Among other things, Roland asked me to keep an eye on a pitcher named Rick Sutcliffe who was about to become a free agent. I told Roland that if Baltimore signed him Sutcliffe would become either their best or their worst pitcher. It all depended on whether the guy's arm would act up. Well, we signed him, and he won 16 games for us. The most satisfying thing about that Sutcliffe deal was that he pitched the first game in the brand-new Camden Yards, a beautiful ballpark that set the standards for all the new parks that would be built in the nineties. The guy shut out Cleveland on five hits.

Cruising with the Team

I had recently retired from the Baltimore club when Roland Hemond called me up to ask if Mary and I would like to go on a cruise. About that time Mary and I needed a break so we decided that we would like it. It was an Orioles cruise into the Caribbean. I don't believe I ever had more fun than we had on that cruise. I had some worries about two old people trying to enjoy the activities that take place on that type of cruise, but it was a cruise of ballplayers, and I discovered that the ballplayers of today are human. They are all millionaires, but they are human.

The Baltimore ballclub had invited Earl Weaver and me and all the rest of the Baltimore front office and a whole mess of retired and active players. It gave all of us a chance to become friendly. In spite of the amount of money these guys were making the players and their wives were just great human beings who could have a great time doing the simple things everybody does on a cruise ship. I think that everybody who took this cruise got a better understanding of one another. Deep down these players are just guys who happened to be lucky enough to be in a sport where they are offered staggering sums of money to play. So what is a guy supposed to say? He says, Yes, I'll take $1 million, or $2 million, or $10 million!

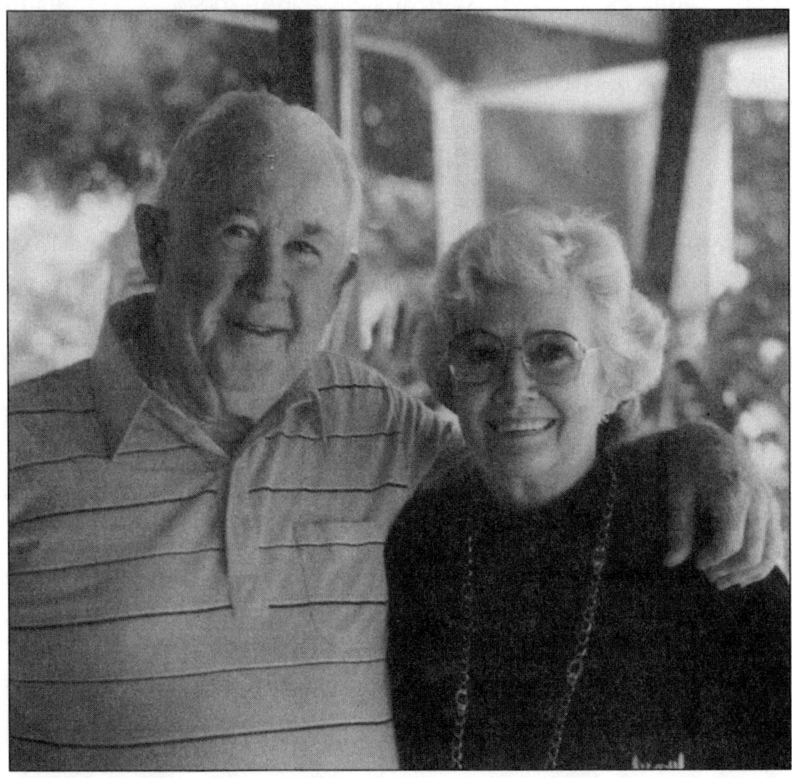

Mary and me in our golden years.

Time Redux

Back to that picture on the cover of *Time.* I don't really know whether or not the *Time* jinx affected my career, but I do know that years later it got me an invitation to a banquet. It was held in Boston at some exclusive club and it was a black-tie affair. Elegant. It was put on by *Time* magazine to honor all those people from New England whose picture had appeared on the cover of the magazine. The people being honored that night were a big collection of scientists, authors, poets, a senator, a Nobel laureate or two, a president of Harvard, the presidents of some big corporations including the guy who invented the Polaroid camera. After cocktails and a four-course dinner a man who I think was the publisher of *Time* got up to speak. He began by telling a few jokes. Then he asked each of the honorees to stand while he read a few words to describe their achievements. And each time he did so there would be applause. Some got more than others, but most of these people had written books you'd heard about or had done things you might have read about in the papers or seen on television. And then he came to me: " George Robert Tebbetts, all-star catcher for the Boston Red Sox and manager . . ." And before the guy could finish, and before I could stand up, a roar went up and all these remarkable gray-haired people were staring at me, standing and clapping and whistling like a bunch of schoolkids. I stood and looked around at these grinning faces, and I nodded and gave a little wave and was embarrassed until it died down.

I'd been booed plenty in the ballpark, and once in a while when I did something well I won some cheers from fans in the stands, but this was up close and personal. It took a few years before it dawned on me what was going on that night in Boston. First, it wasn't so much a tribute to me as it was to the Red Sox. New Englanders have a deep affection for the Red Sox. They just do. And second–and I really think this–I'm sure every person there that night had at one

Susan Tebbetts Mitchell on

Life with Birdie

Toward the end, first of all he wanted his memorabilia straightened out. That was his passion. Hundreds of autographed balls, bats, old uniforms, lineup cards, and who knows what else. Rooms full of stuff. Some in bank vaults. He had been collecting it for 60 years. From the time he retired he always had a project going–getting it together, making sure everybody understood what he had. "Don't screw the thing up. Don't throw stuff out!" He did not want to die until he knew everything was in place.

And then he got too sick, and we got a call from his doctor, who said, "Your father does not have long to live. You need to come over right away." They moved him over to the hospital, and when Pat and I got there George and Betty were standing by the bed. Dad looked around at all of us and said, "What is this? A wedding or a wake? Just tell me the facts. What's going on here?" Until then, nobody had said a word to him. And I had to say, "They called us and said you are going to die, Dad."

The phone rang and it was Joe Garagiola and Roland Hemond calling from Phoenix. He took the phone, listened for a while, and he said, "I'm going down, Joe." And after hanging up he said, "OK, listen. I want you all to be fair to each other. I've got it together. *And don't throw anything out!* Let appraisers see everything. Everything has value." And then he died. He had the flowers from Ted Williams sitting right beside his bed. That meant a lot to him.

[*Author's note:* The estate of George Robert "Birdie" Tebbetts included his baseball memorabilia, which was sold at auction for a sum approaching $1 million, proving that Birdie was not only a collector but a prophet. The proceeds go to the education of his grandchildren.]

time in their life tried like hell to hit a fastball or to throw a curve or slide into second standing up or feel the sting of a line drive hitting their glove. Those were the things, the old childhood memories, that in that moment bound them all together, and those memories came alive when the announcer introduced an old catcher for the Red

Sox. So, in a way, they were just showing their admiration for skills they had yearned to possess as kids. I guess it's that incessant yearning that keeps the game alive.

Life Without Mary

Mary died and I am alone. Before she passed away she once mentioned the sofas made of All-Star bats. We had one in the den and the other we had loaned out to the Cannons, because we didn't have enough room for both in our Milwaukee home. "Why don't you ask the judge to send it back?" she asked. I wanted to forget about the damn things and said that I thought the judge had given it to his son, and after that Mary and I never spoke of it again. So I was alone in the den one day and there was the All-Star-bat sofa, loaded down with books, shoe boxes, and discarded toys. Nobody had sat on it for years. I was suddenly sick of looking at it, so I found a screwdriver and 20 minutes later the next-to-a-last-of-a-kind sofa was a pile of lumber. It fit nicely in the Dumpster behind the bar called the Tip of the Island Bar & Grill, which is a few blocks from my house.

Even though I have an ailment called congestive heart disease and it is pretty hard for me to get around, I can shuffle down to the Tip of the Island most days and sit down and have coffee and talk with these guys while they drink beer.This one bartender knows a lot about baseball so he is good to talk to, and the other guys are always friendly. One time I happened to mention that I could scoot about pretty well in the supermarket when I had one of those shopping carts to lean on. A couple of nights later these guys got drunk, drove 20 miles to a supermarket, and made off with a shopping cart. They put it into their trunk, drove to my house, woke me up at midnight, and made me a present of it. I laughed like hell.

Index

Page references in *italic type* refer to photographs.

C

G

H

N

O

P